PADDINGTON COLLEGE LIBRARY

068251

D0549291

WITHDRAWN

Professional ethics

Tutorial

Jo Osborne

Roger Petheram

osborne BOOKS

CITY OF WESTMINSTER COLLEGE
PADDINGTON LEARNING CENTRE

Date ___ 7 | 3 | 12

Acc. No. 068251

Class No. 657.076 AAT loan

© Jo Osborne, Roger Petheram, 2010. Reprinted 2011.

All rights reserved. No part of this publication may be reproduced, stored in a retrieval system, or transmitted in any form or by any means, electronic, mechanical, photo-copying, recording or otherwise, without the prior consent of the copyright owners, or in accordance with the provisions of the Copyright, Designs and Patents Act 1988, or under the terms of any licence permitting limited copying issued by the Copyright Licensing Agency, Saffron House, 6-10 Kirby Street, London EC1N 8TS.

Published by Osborne Books Limited
Unit 1B Everoak Estate
Bromyard Road
Worcester WR2 5HP
Tel 01905 748071
Email books@osbornebooks.co.uk
Website www.osbornebooks.co.uk

Design by Laura Ingham
Cover and page design image © Istockphoto.com/Petrovich9

Printed by CPI Antony Rowe, Chippenham and Eastbourne

British Library Cataloguing in Publication Data
A catalogue record for this book is available from the British Library

ISBN 978 1905777 341

Contents

Acknowledgements

The authors wish to thank the following for their help with the production of the book: Mike Gilbert, Jon Moore and Cathy Turner. Thanks must also go to Trish Sayer of McKnights of Worcester for advising on current accounting practice and for providing standard letters used in the accounting process.

The publisher is indebted to the Association of Accounting Technicians for its help and advice to our authors and editors during the preparation of this text.

Authors

Jo Osborne is a Chartered Accountant who trained with Ernst & Young in their London office. She then moved to Cable & Wireless where she spent two years in their internal audit department before moving into an investment appraisal role. Jo has taught AAT at Hillingdon College and until recently at Worcester College of Technology where she took on the role of AAT Coordinator.

Roger Petheram has lectured at Worcester College of Technology on a wide range of accounting, business and management courses for a number of years. He previously worked as a senior accountant for the Health Service. He is currently senior editor for accounting texts at Osborne Books, with particular responsibility for the AAT Series.

Introduction

what this book covers

This book has been written specifically to cover the Learning Area 'Professional ethics in accounting and finance' which covers a single QCF Unit in the AAT Level 3 Diploma in Accounting:

■ Professional ethics in accounting and finance

The book may also be used as required by AAT for the Level 2 Certificate in Accounting.

The book contains a clear text with numerous practical examples, chapter summaries and key terms to help with revision. Each chapter has a wide range of student activities in the style of the computer-based assessment.

This book is based on the previous Second edition, with some additions to existing chapters to reflect the new QCF unit. There is also a new chapter on Regulations of the Accounting Profession.

Osborne Workbooks

Osborne Workbooks contain practice material which helps students achieve success in their assessments. *Professional Ethics Workbook* contains a number of paper-based 'fill in' practice exams in the style of the computer-based assessment. Please telephone the Osborne Books Sales Office on 01905 748071 for details of mail ordering, or visit the 24-hour online shop at www.osbornebooks.co.uk

1 Principles of professional ethics

this chapter covers...

The aim of this chapter is to introduce you to the principles of professional ethics. We will look at what 'professional ethics' means and describe the fundamental ethical principles that members of the AAT should follow. These principles are followed in 'Guidelines on Professional Ethics' published by the AAT.

Specific areas covered include:

■ the fundamental principles of professional ethics

■ the people to whom these ethics apply

■ the reasons why professional ethics are necessary

■ the objectives of the accounting profession

AN INTRODUCTION TO PROFESSIONAL ETHICS

what are ethics?

Firstly, a definition:

The professional ethics of an organisation are the moral principles or standards that govern the conduct of the members of that organisation.

You may have heard people refer to the fact that a person or an organisation has done something that is 'unethical', or that they themselves wouldn't do something because it was unethical. For example, you would consider it unethical for a doctor to give information to a newspaper about the treatment given to a celebrity patient without the patient's consent.

So why do we feel that this is unethical on the part of the doctor? In this case the doctor would have broken patient confidentiality – ie released information that is 'secret' and 'private' to that patient – and the doctor's actions would be considered unethical because of this.

Members of professional bodies are expected to maintain the standards of their organisation. As part of this they are expected to behave in a professional and ethical manner. Within the published rules and guidelines of most professional organisations there will be specific sections covering professional ethics. If you have online access, try doing a search on the phrase 'professional ethics for accountants' to appreciate how important the topic is.

professional ethics and the AAT

In the example on the previous page the doctor will be governed by the specific standards of the medical profession in the country in which he/she practises. However, as trainee accountants you are interested in the standards that affect you in your training and when you are qualified. As a professional body the AAT has published the **Guidelines on Professional Ethics** (referred to in this text as the 'Guidelines') which have been designed to help its members maintain the high standard of professionalism that is expected of them.

Decisions made by members of the AAT in their professional life can have real ethical implications. The Guidelines are designed to help members with these decisions. Specifically they state that they:

- set out the expected standard of professional behaviour
- help protect the public interest
- help to maintain the AAT's good reputation

Throughout this book we will examine in detail a number of possible areas where AAT members are faced with ethical dilemmas and we will show how they should be dealt with ethically.

to whom do the AAT Guidelines apply?

The AAT Guidelines on Professional Ethics apply to all fellow, full, affiliate and student members of the AAT. Therefore, as student members you are required to uphold the high professional standards of the AAT even before you have qualified and become a full member.

Some members of the AAT, when they become qualified, will decide to set themselves up in practice rather than continuing to be employed. Whilst the general ethical principles within the accountancy profession will be the same for members whether they are employed in business or in practice, there are a number of different legal and ethical issues that are specific to each group of members.

The AAT has recognised this and has separated the Guidelines into three consecutive parts:

■ Part A applies to **all members**

■ Part B represents additional guidance which applies specifically to **members in practice**

■ Part C applies specifically to **members in business**

what parts of the Guidelines do you need to study?

This Unit requires that you should become very familiar with the AAT Guidelines document. Consequently, even if you currently work as an employee you are still expected to have a clear understanding of professional ethics and be aware of issues raised in the Guidelines.

OBJECTIVES OF THE ACCOUNTING PROFESSION

So far in this chapter we have identified the people who are expected to maintain the professional standards of the AAT with regard to professional ethics, and have described where guidance can be obtained. We will now move on to the objectives of the accounting profession (including the AAT).

The specific objectives of the accounting profession are shown in italics below. Each one is explained separately.

(i) *Mastering of particular skills and techniques acquired through learning and education and maintained through continuing professional development.*

As you will know from your studies, in order to become a member of any of the professional accountancy bodies, individuals must go through a demanding series of exams and assessments. This will normally involve a number of years of study linked to relevant training within the workplace, all of which is designed to ensure that the individual is fully trained to be a member of the accountancy profession and to take on the responsibilities of the role.

In addition to their training, qualified members of all the professional bodies are expected to keep their accounting knowledge up-to-date. This is done through **continuing professional development (CPD)**. As the name suggests, this involves members undertaking activities, such as attending AAT seminars, to keep their knowledge and skills fully up-to-date so that they can carry out their jobs to the highest possible standards. We will look at CPD in more detail in Chapter 2 (page 28).

An example where a member of the accounting profession requires some CPD follows.

> **example**
>
> **the need for CPD**
>
> James Trebor is a member of the AAT and has a successful practice preparing the financial statements of various local businesses. James completed his training in 2002 and although he is competent at what he does, he is not familiar with the new International Accounting Standards (IASs). In order to ensure that the accounts he prepares for his clients comply with the new standards he has obtained copies of the IASs and has also arranged to go on an appropriate course run by the AAT.

(ii) *Development of an ethical approach to the work and to employers and clients, acquired by experience and professional supervision under training and safeguarded by a strict ethical and disciplinary code.*

When training with a professional accountancy body, the most important thing is to pass your exams and assessments and to qualify. However, throughout your training you will also be learning from your supervisors and managers. Whilst this should obviously cover the processes and procedures involved in your job it will also teach you how to approach your work in a professional manner.

Managers who are qualified accountants should 'lead by example' and should ensure that all members of their staff work to the high standards expected of a professional accountant. As part of this they should be demonstrating strong ethical values and ensuring that they maintain the standards of the profession in their work and their dealings with clients.

For example, a manager who tells junior staff that 'it's okay to add a bit extra to their travel expenses claim because everyone does it' is clearly not acting in an ethical manner and is certainly not setting a good example for his or her staff.

(iii) *Acknowledgement of duties to society as a whole in addition to the employer or the client.*

It should be clear that professional accountants have specific duties in relation to their employers and, if they are in practice, in relation to their clients. In addition to this, the accountancy profession understand that they have a duty of care to the general public. Consequently when they are carrying out their work they should always be aware of the wider picture and should consider the implications on society as a whole, as in the example which follows.

example
a duty to society

Whilst preparing the year-end accounts of Flexilock Plc. the accountant, John Bailey, has discovered that the company has been disposing of untreated chemical waste in a local river. John believes that this is illegal.

What should John do with the information that he has obtained?

John is in a difficult situation: he is employed by the company and does not want to risk his job. However as a professional accountant he has a duty to society as a whole, who are likely to be harmed by the actions of the company. Initially John should raise his concerns with someone more senior in the company. If no action is taken John has an obligation to society and should report this information to the relevant authorities.

(iv) *An outlook which is essentially objective, obtained by being fair minded and free from conflicts of interest.*

A person who is **objective** is someone who bases his/her opinions and decisions on real facts and is not influenced by personal beliefs or feelings. Accountants should always be objective. In addition, when they are faced with a conflict of interest, it is their duty not to let their own self-interest – or the interests of the firm that employs them – affect the professional decision that they make. The following example shows how a conflict of interest might arise.

example
a conflict of interest

Jill Saunders is in practice and has been the accountant for Stallone Ltd, a local firm of house builders, for a number of years. The company has two options for its next building project and the directors have asked Jill to draw up a business plan incorporating these options. The directors' preferred option involves purchasing a plot of land directly behind Jill's house and building 20 three and four bedroom houses. Currently Jill has unspoilt views from her house. There is clearly a conflict of interest here. Jill does not want the houses to be built behind her house and consequently can no longer be objective in these circumstances.

It is very important that Jill informs the directors of Stallone as soon as possible of this conflict of interest so that they are then able to make a decision as to whether they wish her to continue to prepare the business plan.

(v)   ***Rendering personal services to the highest standards of conduct and performance.***

This objective can be looked at in two parts. Firstly, accountants must ensure that they carry out every piece of work to the best of their ability. They should allow sufficient time to complete the work, and should never 'cut corners' or compromise on the quality of the work performed. Secondly, accountants should ensure that they have the necessary skills to perform the work being undertaken. The following example shows how this objective may be compromised.

example

highest standards of conduct and performance compromised

Jasmine Chang was asked to prepare the accounts for Blue Truck Ltd. The Finance Director has asked that they be made available for the board meeting in two weeks time. Jasmine agreed to this timescale; however since then two junior members of her staff have been unwell and so have been unable to work. This has meant that Jasmine has had to prepare the accounts herself in addition to her own work.

Just before the board meeting the Finance Director noticed that the accounts appeared to contain a number of errors. He pointed this out to Jasmine who explained that she had been unable to check the detail in the accounts due to the pressures on her time. She knew that she should have spoken to the Finance Director as soon as she realised that the quality of her work might be affected by the shortage of time available to her to complete the assignment.

(vi)   ***Achieving acceptance by the public that members provide accountancy services in accordance with these high standards and requirements.***

The accountancy profession is very focused on ensuring the highest standards from all its members. There is also the objective that accountants should be seen by members of the public to be working to achieve these high standards. In order for this to happen, the perception of the public must be that accountants are professional and trustworthy.

In recent years there have been a number of high profile cases where the standard of work that accountants have carried out has been called into question. The most famous of these is probably the collapse of the American energy company Enron. In 2002 the auditors of Enron, Arthur Andersen, were found guilty of obstruction of justice when there was evidence that they had shredded relevant documents immediately before the firm's collapse. Although this conviction was later overturned, the general public's perception of the accountancy profession was severely damaged by what they saw as highly unethical behaviour on the part of Arthur Andersen.

We can see from these six points that the accountancy profession, including the AAT, has set a number of demanding objectives for its members to commit to. In the next section we will describe how members can ensure that they achieve these objectives wherever possible.

FUNDAMENTAL PRINCIPLES

In order to achieve the objectives of the accountancy profession that have been explained above, a professional accountant is required to comply with a number of fundamental principles. Each of these is explained below, with practical examples. It is important to realise that many of the issues regarding professional ethics cannot be looked at on their own, but should be seen collectively. Where ethical issues arise, a number of the fundamental principles may be involved in any one particular case.

These fundamental principles can be remembered using the letters PPCIO, which also stands for 'Popular People Chat in Offices'. They are explained in the text that follows the diagram.

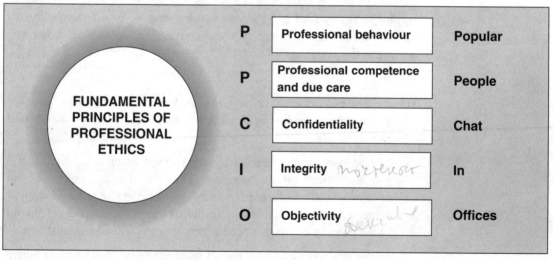

P	Professional behaviour	Popular
P	Professional competence and due care	People
C	Confidentiality	Chat
I	Integrity	In
O	Objectivity	Offices

FUNDAMENTAL PRINCIPLES OF PROFESSIONAL ETHICS

Integrity is the quality of being honest and having strong moral principles that you refuse to compromise. An accountant should be straightforward and honest in performing professional work and in all business relationships.

The following situation is an example of where the integrity of an accountant might be tested.

example

a question of integrity

It is the end of the financial year and the Managing Director has told the Chief Accountant that he wants to maximise the profit for the year. He has asked the Chief Accountant not to set up a provision for doubtful debts of £60,000 against an outstanding amount that the Chief Accountant knows is unlikely to ever be paid as the customer has recently gone into liquidation.

Clearly in this situation the accountant is faced with a difficult decision. He is employed by the company and consequently has a duty to the Managing Director. However, he knows that in order for the accounts to show the true position the debt should be provided against. In order to maintain his integrity in this situation the Chief Accountant should explain to the Managing Director that he is not prepared to ignore the bad debt and that in his opinion it should be provided for in the accounts.

Integrity also involves the personal qualities of **fairness**, **honesty** and **sensitivity**. The AAT guidelines refer to the need for members to act fairly, honestly and with sensitivity. Members must ensure that they deal with colleagues, clients, customers and suppliers **fairly** and with respect and do not discriminate again anyone. **Honesty** means that a member must be truthful and not mislead others. This extends to all aspects of a member's working life regardless of how serious the matter is: leaving work an hour early to watch the football on TV and claiming the reason to be a dental appointment is not acting **honestly** or with **integrity**.

Members must act with **sensitivity** when dealing with colleagues or subordinates. Accountants have a duty of confidentiality to their employers and clients but this must also extend to the people that they work with. Accountants must be sensitive and respect the confidentiality of others that they work with. This is all part of the principle of **integrity**.

objectivity

As a professional accountant the need to remain objective at all times is very important (see also page 6). This means that any decisions that are made should be based on real facts and should not be influenced by personal beliefs or feelings. The accountant must not let his/her own bias or prejudice or pressure from others affect decisions that he/she makes. Essentially, he/she must always act fairly and sensitively and without bias.

An example where the objectivity of an accountant could be affected is illustrated on the next page.

donation political party

> **example**
>
> **a question of objectivity**
>
> Paula Gradwell is a senior accountant with a small local firm and is currently working on the year-end accounts of Bell & Sons. The owner, Alexander Bell, has asked Paula for her advice on whether the company should make a donation to the political party that he personally supports and how this will be treated in the financial statements. Paula has strong personal views against the party in question.
>
> In this situation Paula must ensure that she remains objective when providing Alexander with advice. She must explain to him how any donation that Bell & Sons makes should be disclosed in the company's accounts. In this situation she must not let her personal opinions affect the advice that she gives.

professional competence and due care

If we first look at **Professional Competence**; professional accountants have a duty to keep themselves up-to-date with developments in the accounting profession, including relevant (international) accounting or auditing standards, and also regulatory and statutory requirements. The way in which they are expected to do this is by completing continuing professional development (CPD) on a regular basis, by reading current information on technical developments in the profession or attending relevant training courses. The topic of CPD will be developed further in Chapter 2.

The influence of international accounting standards is a specific example of the need for professional accountants to update their technical knowledge through training courses run by their own professional bodies.

Ideally, professional accountants should only take on new assignments for which they already have the necessary professional and technical skills. However, in certain circumstances, they may take on new work for which they will need some additional help or advice, as in the following example.

> **example**
>
> **VAT expertise**
>
> One of your firm's clients has asked you to provide specific advice on the VAT implications of a new product imported from overseas. Although you have come across VAT as part of your AAT studies it is not something with which you feel particularly comfortable. So, what options are open to you in this situation?

1 You could decline the assignment on the basis that you are not suitably competent to carry out the work involved

2 You could employ someone with the appropriate skills to complete the work you cannot do, or subcontract the parts of the assignment you are unable to undertake

3 You could arrange appropriate training for yourself to enable you to carry out the VAT work that the client has requested

In each of the three options above as a professional accountant you are ensuring that the work carried out is performed to the highest standards, either by someone else, or by you with additional training.

The second part of this principle is **Due Care.** This means that when carrying out an assignment an accountant must always take the appropriate amount of care (ie '**due care**') to ensure that the quality of the work performed meets the high standards expected of the accounting profession. Each assignment must be assessed individually in relation to its importance to the client and the time allowed for its completion. Whilst the work should be completed as quickly as is reasonably possible this should not compromise its quality.

Accountants must take particular care where clients are totally unfamiliar with anything to do with accounting or taxation. In such circumstances, accountants must be very careful to ensure that they carry out their work to the required standard. In addition to this they must also ensure that they explain fully to the client the results of the work that they have performed and the implications that this may have for the client.

For example, if two sole traders who do not seem to know much about accounting or taxation approach a professional accountant for financial advice as to whether they should go into partnership together, the accountant must ensure that he/she makes each of them fully aware of all the taxation and accounting implications involved.

confidentiality

At the start of the chapter we introduced the example of a doctor who broke his patient's confidentiality by passing information to the press. All professions need to maintain confidentiality of client information. Accountants accumulate a large amount of information about their clients' affairs in the course of their work. Only in the most serious of circumstances, where there is a legal duty to disclose, would accountants be justified in revealing confidential information about their clients.

The example on the next page raises the issue of confidentiality.

example

a question of confidentiality

You work for an accounting practice with a large number of clients in the local area. One Friday evening you have dinner with a good friend who explains that he has been offered a job with a local firm of publishers. He knows that they are one of your firm's clients and over dinner he asks you what their financial position is like and whether you feel that it would be a good move for him.

How should you deal with his questions?

In order to maintain the confidentiality of your client you should not disclose any information that is not already in the public domain. You should explain the need for confidentiality to your friend. You could suggest that he get the latest set of published accounts from Companies House which would give him an idea of the financial position of the company.

The subject of confidentiality and examples of situations when it can be broken are covered in detail in Chapter 3 (pages 36- 48).

professional behaviour

The final fundamental principle is that of professional behaviour.

As we have seen earlier in this chapter the accountancy profession is respected for the high standards that it requires of its members. Therefore, members must always ensure that they do not bring the profession into disrepute by acting in any way which is unprofessional or does not comply with relevant laws and regulations.

For example, a member of the AAT who sends offensive or inappropriate emails from their place of work would be considered unprofessional. In addition this could reflect very badly on the firm that he works for and also on the AAT.

A much more serious example of a member damaging the reputation of the accountancy profession would be if he or she gave professional advice to a client that the member knew failed to comply with relevant laws and regulations.

Chapter Summary	■ Members of all professional accounting bodies should maintain the standards of that organisation.

■ Members of all professional accounting bodies should maintain the standards of that organisation.

■ The professional ethics of an organisation are the moral principles or standards that govern the conduct of its members.

■ The Guidelines on Professional Ethics issued by the AAT give its members guidance in situations where ethical conflicts arise.

■ The Guidelines on Professional Ethics document is split into three sections:
  - general principles, applicable to all members
  - guidance specifically for employed members
  - guidance for members in practice

■ The Guidelines state that the accountancy profession (including the AAT) is committed to six objectives:
  - mastering skills and techniques through learning and training
  - developing an ethical approach to work and observing a code of ethics
  - acknowledging a duty to society as a whole
  - adopting an objective approach, free from conflicts of interest
  - providing accounting services to the highest standards
  - ensuring that the public knows that accountants provide services to these high standards

■ In order to achieve these objectives all members should observe the fundamental principles listed below.

  The Guidance sets out five fundamental principles:
  - integrity
  - objectivity
  - professional competence and due care
  - confidentiality
  - professional behaviour

Key Terms		
	professional ethics	the moral principles or standards that govern the conduct of the members of an organisation
	Guidelines on Professional Ethics	A document issued by the AAT providing guidance to full and student members regarding professional ethics
	integrity	members should be straightforward and honest in performing professional duties
	continuing professional development	members of professional accounting bodies are expected to keep their technical knowledge up-to-date through relevant study, training and by attending courses
	objectivity	decisions should be made based on true facts and accountants must not let their own bias or prejudice, or pressure from others affect decisions that they make
	conflict of interest	these arise where the business or personal interests of a member may intervene to prevent the member giving an objective opinion
	professional competence and due care	members have a duty to ensure that they have the necessary skills to carry out any work that is assigned to them and that they always take sufficient care to ensure that the quality of their work meets the high standards expected of them
	confidentiality	information obtained during the course of professional work should not be disclosed without proper and specific authority or unless there is a legal duty to do so
	professional behaviour	accountants should maintain the good reputation of the profession and should not do anything to discredit the profession

Activities

1.1   The AAT Guidelines on Professional Ethics apply to which category of members in the following list? You may tick as many categories as you wish.

	✔
Full AAT members	✓
Student members of the AAT	✓
Members who work in practice	✓
Members who are employed in industry	✓

1.2   Which one of the following is an objective of the accounting profession?

	✔
Maintaining acceptable accounting skills to ensure reasonable standards of performance	✓
Rendering personal services to the highest standards of conduct and performance	
Acknowledging a duty to the clients or employer above all others	

1.3   The abbreviation CPD stands for which of the following?

	✔
Continuing Personal Development	
Continued Professional Diligence	
Continuing Professional Development	✓

1.4   Which one of the following is not one of the five Fundamental Principles of Professional Ethics?

	✔
Integrity	
Confidentiality	
Trustworthiness	✓
Professional competence and due care	

1.5   Complete the following sentence by selecting the appropriate option from the list below:

Basing decisions on real facts rather than being influenced by personal beliefs or feelings is following the fundamental ethical principle of ....

	✔
Integrity	
Objectivity	✓
Professional behaviour	

1.6   Rebecca works for an accounting practice. Her sister Simone is going for an interview with a local firm of chartered surveyors which is a client of Rebecca's firm. Simone telephones Rebecca and asks her for information on the financial position of the chartered surveyors and if she has any useful personal information about the partner who will be conducting the interview.

Which of the following fundamental principles does this compromise? (tick any that you feel apply)

	✔
Integrity	✓
Professional competence and due care	
Confidentiality	✓
Objectivity	✓

for your notes

Objectivity and professional competence

This chapter explains the practical approach that the AAT takes to professional ethics and looks in more detail at objectivity and the need for an accountant to be independent. The chapter also deals with the way in which ethical problems can be resolved and finally covers the ways in which accountants ensure that they are sufficiently competent to carry out their work.

Specific areas covered include:

■ *the difference between a conceptual framework and a rule-based approach to professional ethics*

■ *the principles of objectivity and independence*

■ *how to resolve ethical conflict*

■ *presentation of information*

■ *attaining and maintaining professional competence*

A CONCEPTUAL FRAMEWORK APPROACH

what are the principles?

Chapter 1 of this book covered the fundamental principles of professional ethics. You may remember the mnemonic: **P**opular **P**eople **C**hat **I**n **O**ffices. This will remind you of the five fundamental principles of professional ethics:

■ **P**rofessional Competence and Due Care

■ **P**rofessional Behaviour

■ **C**onfidentiality

■ **I**ntegrity

■ **O**bjectivity

The AAT believes that its members should take a conceptual framework approach to professional ethics. This means that when faced with ethical decisions members should consider their decisions based on these fundamental principles rather than using a rigid system of rules and regulations.

We have seen that these principles are general in nature and so cannot be applied rigidly in specific situations to solve ethical problems that members come across in their working lives. When ethical dilemmas occur these principles should be considered together with the **Guidelines on Professional Ethics** ('Guidelines') produced by the AAT. Members should use their judgement and make all necessary enquiries before any decision is reached on ethical matters.

conceptual framework approach

The AAT states that members should take a conceptual framework approach to ethics which means that you look at the objective that is to be achieved and focus on that objective rather than applying the rules exactly as stated regardless of the circumstances (ie literally), which would be a rules-based approach.

Put simply, this means that AAT members, where possible, should look at the objective to be achieved and focus on that objective rather than sticking rigidly to a set of rules.

The difference between a principle-based approach and a rule-based approach can be seen in the example that now follows.

example

conceptual framework approach v rule-based approach

Your firm of accountants has recently been taken on to provide professional accounting services for James Roberts, who is a self-employed painter and decorator. When preparing James's end of year accounts you realise that, early on in the year, the business's turnover has exceeded the annual limit for Valued Added Tax (VAT). This means that James should have registered for VAT and should from that point have been charging VAT on his services.

What should you do in this situation?

Taking a rule-based approach you would report James to HMRC for failing to register for VAT when his business had reached the VAT limit. This would arguably be a harsh course of action.

The preferred conceptual framework approach, on the other hand, would involve explaining to James that he must register for VAT immediately and should also make HM Revenue and Customs (HMRC) aware of the delay in registering that has occurred and the fact that he has not charged VAT on his services during the year as he should have done. Using this approach, you have identified the main issue – which is that James registers for VAT as soon as possible – and you have given James the necessary professional advice to allow him to do so.

OBJECTIVITY

what is objectivity?

One of the fundamental principles covered in Chapter 1 is **objectivity,** which should be maintained at all times. A person who is objective has already been defined in Chapter 1 as someone who bases his/her opinions and decisions on real facts and is not influenced by personal beliefs or feelings or those of other people. It is also important for an accountant to ensure that he/she collects all the information that is required before making any judgements.

If we now look at objectivity in more detail we can identify the key points that ensure that an accountant remains objective.

Firstly, in order to remain objective, an accountant should treat every situation equally and ensure that every point of view is given equal consideration (fair-minded). In addition to this the accountant should gather, analyse and present information accurately. To remain objective all members need to be free from conflicts of interest. This means that they must not allow their own self-interest or that of the organisation that they work for to influence any decision that they make.

independence

The principle of objectivity goes hand-in-hand with the need for independence. A definition of independence is **'freedom from control or influence of others'.**

An accountant must always carry out his/her work in an independent way and regardless of any external pressure. There may be people who try to put pressure on an accountant, or even make threats to try to ensure that the accountant's work is performed to best suit their needs. In order to act in a professional and ethical manner the accountant must not be influenced by this pressure and must remain independent.

example

a question of independence

Amerdeep Johal works for a firm of accountants and is currently preparing the year-end accounts for ABP Supplies, a local company owned by two brothers Andrew and Brian Potter. Amerdeep has calculated a draft profit figure for the year of £56,000 compared with £127,000 in the previous year. During a meeting with the two brothers Andrew says that he is not happy with this profit figure as he has a meeting with the bank at the end of the week to discuss a loan and he knows they will be unhappy with such a large drop in profit. He asks

Amerdeep if there is any way that he could 'improve' the profit figure.

Amerdeep explains that this would not be appropriate as the accounts would no longer give an accurate picture of the financial state of affairs of the business. Andrew replies that he will need to speak to the partner in the firm that Amerdeep works for who is a close friend of his and if this is not resolved he may consider changing the firm of accountants that ABP Supplies uses.

In this situation Amerdeep is being pressured by Andrew. Firstly, he will feel personal pressure as Andrew has threatened to speak to Amerdeep's boss. Secondly, he has threatened to take his business elsewhere which will have an impact on the firm that Amerdeep works for. In order to remain independent Amerdeep should not allow these pressures to influence him. He must stick to his principles and, provided his boss has the same ethical principles, Amerdeep should be confident that he will support him and will not expect Amerdeep to change his opinion.

In stressing the importance for members to remain independent, the AAT state that members must be both **independent of mind** and **independent in appearance**. We will now describe what is meant by these.

independence of mind

This means that when carrying out work and making decisions, a professional accountant should only take into account points and issues which are relevant to the job that he or she is doing. This is more or less the same as the principle of objectivity which we have discussed above. But in addition to being objective the accountant must be able to come to an opinion without his/her professional judgement being compromised.

independence in appearance

In addition to maintaining objectivity and independence, an accountant must ensure that he/she is **seen to be** independent. This means that any reasonable person who comes into contact with the accountant must be confident that he/she always behaves independently and has avoided doing anything that may bring that independence into question.

The following example highlights a situation that may affect the **independence in appearance** of a professional accountant.

example

independence in appearance

Ashton and Groves is a small firm of accountants in Broom Town. One of the partners, Jemima Ashton, is married to Frank, who owns a local car dealership, Ashton Motors. For many years Ashton Motors have used

Edwards & Co, another firm of accountants in the town, to prepare their year-end accounts. But Jim Edwards has just retired and Edwards & Co have ceased to operate.

Frank has suggested that the obvious solution would be for Ashton and Groves to take on the preparation of Ashton Motors accounts. But would this be appropriate?

The answer is no. Jemima, one of the Ashton & Groves partners, is clearly linked to the car dealership because she is married to Frank, its owner. Even if she had no involvement in the preparation of the accounts for Ashton Motors, her close personal relationship with Frank means that any outsider could quite justifiably question the independence and objectivity of Ashton and Groves.

safeguarding independence and objectivity

There are a number of factors that will influence an accountant and safeguard his/her independence and objectivity.

- Throughout their training professional accountants have been taught to act in a professional and ethical manner. They will be able to identify situations that could potentially affect their independence and they will be able to deal effectively with threats or pressures exerted on them.

- An accountant should be aware of the possibility of legal action if he/she gives in to pressures that are exerted and allows his/her independence to be compromised.

- Members of any one of the professional accounting bodies such as AAT, CIMA or ACCA, are aware of the possibility of professional disciplinary procedures against them from these bodies if they do not remain independent at all times.

- Finally, if an accountant is found to have compromised his/her objectivity and independence, this could potentially damage the accountant's reputation. The loss of professional reputation will often lead to the loss of clients and ultimately to loss of earnings.

acceptance of gifts

One possible threat to the independence of an accountant is the acceptance of gifts, services, favours or hospitality from a client. This is because there is a risk that these gifts could influence the work performed and decisions made by the accountant, effectively by bribing the accountant.

The problem here is whether all gifts should be refused or whether it is acceptable to receive certain small gifts and favours. There is an argument that accepting a bottle of wine or some chocolates from a client at Christmas will not influence an accountant's work or opinions. However, would this still be the case if the gift was a case of wine? At what point would it no longer be appropriate to accept such gifts?

The following example illustrates this issue.

example

Merry Christmas!

Simon Fuller works for Adams & Co, a firm of accountants in Bridgetown. During the week before Christmas, Sara, one of the owners of Peroni, a local restaurant which is one of the firm's clients, turns up at the office with a crate of champagne. Sara hands it to Simon together with a Christmas card and wishes him a Happy Christmas. She suggests that he gives a bottle to each member of staff. Sara says 'tell Roger Adams that I've arranged the table for your firm's Christmas party on Friday and not to worry about the bill as it's on Peroni!'

What are the ethical implications of this situation? Should Simon Fuller accept the champagne and should Adams & Co accept the offer of a free Christmas meal from Peroni?

With regard to the champagne it is unlikely that if each member of staff accepts a bottle of champagne this will influence their independence when working on the accounts of Peroni. The acceptance of a free Christmas meal, however, is another matter. This is likely to mean a substantial cost saving for Adams & Co. If a third party was aware of this they may consider that Adams & Co could be influenced by the financial benefit that they are getting by not paying for the meal. Even if the owners of Peroni say that they do not expect anything in return, Adams & Co should decline the offer, enjoy the meal and ensure that they pay for it in full.

From this example it can be seen that there are no rules regarding what is and what is not acceptable. A professional accountant must use professional judgement and experience to decide whether he or she is allowed to accept gifts from a client. In most cases, however, if there is any question in the accountant's mind he or she should politely refuse a gift from a client.

PREPARATION AND REPORTING OF INFORMATION

Accountants are often involved in the preparation and reporting of financial and management information. The AAT expects its members to prepare and present financial information 'fairly, honestly and in accordance with professional standards so that it will be understood in its context'. This means that they should disclose all relevant figures and supporting documentation without bias and in a way that the reader can understand clearly.

Members of the AAT must ensure that when they prepare financial information they remember the needs of the users and always ensure that the information that they present is a true reflection of the financial state of affairs of the business.

In addition to this, accountants must prepare this information in accordance with accepted accounting standards.

The example that follows demonstrates the need for clear presentation of financial information.

example

the value of chocolate

You are assistant accountant for Top Chocs, a company which supplies quality boxes of chocolates to retail stores. It is the end of February and you have been included in the team to perform the annual stock count for the year ended 28 February. This involves counting all the stock that is held on the company's premises, checking it to the stock records and placing an accurate value on it.

During the stock count you discover 20 crates which each contain 500 boxes of Christmas chocolates. When you check the stock records you find that these chocolates are still being valued at the full cost. By the time next Christmas comes these chocolates will no longer be edible and are realistically now only fit to be sold at a heavily discounted price.

In order to ensure that the accounts give a true picture of the state of the company's financial affairs these items of stock must be valued in accordance with the appropriate accounting standards – in this case SSAP 9, 'Stock and work in progress' or the international equivalent IAS 2 'Inventories'. These both state that stock should be valued at the lower of cost and net realisable value. Therefore the stock must be written down in the financial statements to whatever value it can be sold for.

RESOLUTION OF ETHICAL CONFLICTS

This book aims to explain how professional ethics affect the working lives of members of the accountancy profession. In order to illustrate this, many of the examples that have been used throughout this book involve situations where the accountant is faced with an ethical conflict. Some of the issues may be relatively minor. In some cases, however, an accountant may be faced with more serious matters such as fraud or other illegal activities.

There are various cases where a member may be under serious pressure to behave in a way that conflicts with the fundamental ethics principles we have looked at in Chapter 1. Two particularly serious issues are:

■ pressure to act illegally

■ pressure to act contrary to technical or professional standards

These two points are each explained separately below and illustrated with a brief example.

pressure to act illegally

A member should not under any circumstances do anything that is illegal. If a client or colleague asks or tells them to do something that is against the law, false or dishonest they must refuse.

example

making bread – a question of pay

You have recently been offered the job as the accountant for Frankley and Peters, a local firm that runs a small chain of bakeries. Part of your duties is to prepare the payroll for all staff. Janet Peters tells you that the company pays all their staff a basic wage on which PAYE and National Insurance Contributions (NICs) are paid – the remainder is paid in cash.

What should you do?

This practice is illegal as all earnings should be taken into account when calculating and paying PAYE and NICs. Consequently you should tell Janet that you are not prepared to carry on with this practice and that you will not be able to accept the position unless all wages are correctly accounted for by the business.

pressure to act contrary to technical or

professional standards

If an accountant is faced with a situation where he/she is being asked to do something that does not comply with technical standards, for example accounting standards, or professional standards, such as the ethical standards set out in the AAT Guidelines, they must not do so.

example

client list confidentiality

You work for a small firm of accountants which has recently taken on a new member of staff. She explains that she is still in touch with some of her old colleagues from her previous place of work and could easily get you a copy of their client list. This would then in her words 'give you a readymade list of potential new clients to approach, especially as I know what these clients are currently paying their accountants.'

Would it be appropriate to accept this offer?

This is a clear breach of confidentiality on the part of your new employee. Approaching these clients on this basis is not acceptable and could result in the other firm taking legal action against your firm. In this situation you should explain to the new member of staff that this is extremely unethical and cannot be considered in any circumstances.

difference of opinion

There are also situations where there could be potential for ethical conflict but in actual fact it is no more than an honest difference of opinion between the accountant and another person.

If an accountant disagrees with a client or colleague this is not necessarily an ethical conflict, provided the disagreement is an honest one and the viewpoint of each side is valid. It becomes an ethical conflict when the accountant believes that the opinion or action of the client or colleague is unethical or unlawful.

example

a question of value

You work as the Financial Accountant for Snax, a biscuit manufacturer. It is the end of the financial year and you and the Financial Controller are discussing the valuation of year end stock. The Financial Controller believes that stock should be valued at the average cost (AVCO) whereas you prefer the more prudent approach of valuing stock using First in Fist out (FIFO).

Is there an ethical issue in this situation?

Under Standard Statement of Accounting Practice 9 (and IAS 2) both AVCO and FIFO are acceptable methods of valuing stock. Therefore, whilst there is clearly a difference of opinion between you and the Financial Controller, there is no question that any action taken by the Financial Controller would be unethical or unlawful.

resolving ethical conflicts

If an accountant believes that a significant ethical conflict has arisen from any pressure that has been put on him/her there are steps that he/she can take to deal with it. These include:

■ obtaining advice from his/her employer, an independent professional advisor or a professional body

- using the formal dispute process with the organisation who employs him/her
- seeking professional advice

Each of these highlights the point that a professional accountant should know when to ask for advice. When AAT members come up against a potential ethical problem that they do not feel confident dealing with they should either take legal advice or they should contact the AAT Ethics Advice Line.

---

example

finding a fraud - taking advice

Your boss is away on holiday and you have been asked to cover his job for the next two weeks. Whilst carrying out his job it becomes apparent to you that he has been making unauthorised payments from the company bank account into his own personal account without any supporting documentation.

What should you do in this situation?

Your immediate reaction would probably be to report him to his manager. However, there is always the risk that his manager could also be involved in the potential fraud. It may be more appropriate in this situation to seek advice from a third party. This could be from a solicitor or from the AAT Ethics Advice Line. It is quite likely that the advice they give will be to report the matter to the senior management of the business, but it is always worth seeking advice if you are unsure in a situation such as this.

---

keeping written records

When a member of the AAT is faced with an ethical conflict it is very important to make sure that he/she keeps a note of all meetings and discussions that are held to try and resolve the conflict. This will include details of who attended the meeting, what was discussed and any decisions that were reached. One of the main reasons for this is that this will act as proof if ever the accountant is faced with legal proceedings.

---

example

finding a fraud - keeping records

Consider again the example shown above ('finding a fraud - taking advice') where your boss has been found to be defrauding the company. In this situation you must always ensure that you keep a written record of discussions you have had with solicitors or the AAT Ethics Advice Line as proof that you have taken steps to resolve the ethical conflict with which you have been faced. If and when you report the matter to senior management within your organisation you must also ensure that all meetings and discussions are accurately recorded.

The issue of ethical conflict is also related to the issue of 'Conflict of loyalties' which will be covered in Chapter 4 (for employed members) and Chapter 5 (for members in practice).

The key issues that have emerged over the last few pages are that members of the accounting profession should never do anything that they believe to be illegal or unethical; where they are faced with an ethical conflict that they cannot resolve they should seek advice from a solicitor or from the AAT Ethics Advice Line.

PROFESSIONAL COMPETENCE

Before taking on a new client or a new piece of work, an accountant must make sure that he/she has the ability to carry out the work involved and the necessary professional competence to complete the job.

There are two separate issues which relate to a member's competence. First of all, a member must gain (attain) professional competence. Secondly, a member must ensure that he/she maintains professional competence. We will now explain each of these in turn.

attainment of professional competence

Most people who are reading this book will be studying to become a member of the AAT and will probably be working in an accounting related job. By the time all the training, assessment and examinations have been successfully completed to allow a person to become a member of the AAT this should mean that they have gained the necessary professional competence.

maintenance of professional competence

This is not, however, the end of the training for a professional accountant. Regardless of the professional body which has awarded the qualification, there is a requirement to maintain a level of professional competence. Members must keep up-to-date with all new developments in the accounting profession: as you know from your studies in other units accounting standards are changing both nationally and internationally. Accountants are required to keep up-to-date with all these changes, together with any other relevant amendments to auditing standards or other legislation such as changes in taxation laws.

The preferred way for members of the AAT to maintain professional competence is through **continued professional development (CPD)**. This is learning that accountants need to carry out to stay competent so that they are effective and successful throughout their chosen career.

The AAT Council recommends that its members should follow a programme of relevant continuing professional development (CPD) each year. CPD used to be measured in hours. However, it is now measured by the outcomes and benefits the members get from doing CPD.

AAT CPD CYCLE

The AAT CPD policy requires that members in practice undertake sufficient CPD to ensure their competence to carry out the services that they are licensed to provide. Part of this requirement is to go through the CPD cycle at least twice in a 12 month period. The CPD cycle consists of four stages:

- assess
- plan
- action
- evaluate

We will now look briefly at what is involved at each stage.

assess

In this step of the CPD cycle the member should start by asking the following questions:

- what are my CPD goals?
- what must I learn to achieve my goals?
- what can I do well and where could I improve?
- are there any particular gaps in my skill set that I can prioritise?

By answering these questions the member will identify the areas which he/she needs to focus on for professional development.

plan

Once the member has identified the areas he/she needs to develop it is time to work out how to fill this gap in his/her skills. The AAT have an extensive CPD zone on their website, https://www.aat.org.uk/myaat/cpd_zone/, which includes a 'CPD planner template' that members can use to plan out the continuing professional development that they are going to undertake. At this stage the questions to ask are:

- what do I need to do to meet my goals?
- how does this fit with the resources I have available, in terms of time and money?

- what kind of learning do I respond to best?

- do I prefer on-the-job training, attending courses or e-learning?

By answering these questions members can decide what type of development they can afford to undertake in terms of the cost and the time that they can dedicate to it. They can then arrange the necessary training to undertake.

action

At this point in the CPD cycle the member can stop asking themselves questions and actually 'take action'. In simple terms this means carry out the plan. This may be through attending training courses, obtaining on the job training from experienced colleagues, self study, research etc. A full list of possible CPD activities is detailed below at the end of this section.

Because the AAT expect its members to record the CPD that they achieve it is useful to write down anything new that has been learned. This will make it much easier to fill in the CPD records that need to be sent to the AAT. As a member you do not have to limit the CPD that you record to formal training courses, you can also include informal learning which has helped you to do your job more effectively.

evaluate

Once the CPD activity has been carried out by the member he/she must evaluate whether it has been worthwhile and assess the benefits that he/she has gained.

Evaluation can be seen in two parts. Firstly on a basic level was the activity worth the time and money that the member spent on it? Secondly, the member needs to reflect on how the CPD fits into his/her overall development and whether it means that he/she can carry out his/her work more effectively.

At this stage the final set of questions that need to be asked are:

- how useful has my learning been?

- do I feel better equipped for my current role as a result?

- have I achieved the goals I set myself?

- are there any goals that remain which can be carried forward to my next CPD plan?

Going through this cycle twice a year will focus a member of the AAT on what development needs he/she has and how best to achieve them. By maintaining effective CPD this will also ensure that the professional competence of the member will be maintained together with an ethical approach to his/her work.

The following are specific examples of appropriate CPD that have been identified by the AAT, however any learning, training or experience that helps you do your job or develop your career counts as CPD.

- workshops, training courses, conferences

- AAT or other professional body branch/society meetings

- planned coaching from colleagues or specialists

- structured discussion groups

- studying for further qualifications

- on-line/CD-Rom courses

- planned reading/research

- using audio, video or IT resources

- special project work or job secondment

- hands-on development of skills (eg IT or presentations)

- membership of local or professional groups

- voluntary work

With all the choices above, it would seem very straightforward for an accountant to achieve the required amount of CPD. However, it is very important to stress that the CPD that is undertaken by the accountant must be relevant, and significant learning must take place. For example attending a local AAT meeting is only relevant CPD if the subjects discussed are relevant to the accountant's job. Similarly, acting voluntarily as treasurer for a local cricket club may be relevant CPD but working on a Saturday morning as a dog walker at the local dog shelter may not be!

Chapter Summary

- When ethical decisions need to be taken, a conceptual framework approach should be adopted, based on the objective to be achieved rather than applying the rules exactly as stated.

- Accountants must follow the principle of objectivity which is key to professional accountants remaining independent.

- When making decisions, an accountant must ensure that he/she remains independent of mind and only take into account issues and points that are relevant to the issues that they are addressing.

- In addition to independence of mind, the accountant must demonstrate independence in appearance. This means that they should avoid situations that could make a third party question the accountant's objectivity.

- A professional accountant must use his or her professional judgement to decide whether to accept gifts from a client.

- When an accountant prepares financial information it should be presented fully, honestly and professionally and should clearly describe the true nature of business transactions, assets and liabilities.

- Where ethical conflicts arise, accountants should take all necessary steps to resolve these, and if necessary should seek advice from a solicitor or from the AAT Ethics Advice Line.

- Members of the AAT and other professional accountants should only accept new work if they are professionally competent to carry it out.

- A member attains professional competence through training and qualifying as an accountant.

- To maintain professional competence members of the AAT and other professional accounting bodies should undertake the CPD cycle twice a year.

Key Terms	**conceptual framework approach**	the approach to professional ethics that means you look at the objective that is to be achieved and focus on that objective
	rule-based approach	the approach to professional ethics that means that you apply any rules exactly as stated regardless of the circumstances
	objectivity	not allowing personal beliefs or feelings or pressure from others to affect decisions that are made
	independence of mind	only taking into account points that are relevant to decisions to be made or work that is being undertaken – this is very similar to objectivity
	independence in appearance	ensuring that to a third party the actions taken by the accountant appear to be objective and free from the influence of others
	ethical conflict	this occurs where there is a fundamental disagreement between what has been requested of the accountant and what his/her ethical principles indicate that he/she should do
	professional competence	the necessary skills and expertise to carry out existing or new assignments to the required standards
	continuing professional development (CPD)	members of professional accounting bodies are expected to keep their technical knowledge up-to-date through relevant study and training, and by attending appropriate courses
	CPD cycle	maintaining CPD through the cycle of assessing, planning, taking action and evaluating

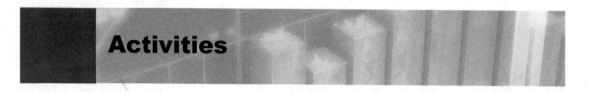

Activities

2.1 The conceptual framework approach to ethics requires members to:

~~just one benefit~~

A   Follow a set of rules laid down in the AAT guidelines

B   Look at the objective that is to be achieved and focus on that objective ✓

Choose one of the above options.

2.2 'Freedom from the control or influence of others' is one definition of which of the following:

	✔
Conflict of interest	
Independence	
Objectivity	✓

2.3 Choose the appropriate words from the selection below to complete the following sentence.

Members of the AAT should be both independent of ....*mind*........and independent in .....*appearance*......

mind •   **spirit**   **thought**   **appearance**   **outlook**

2.4 Members of the AAT are permitted to accept gifts from clients provided the gift is worth less than £20?

True or (False?)

2.5 Members should use their professional judgement to decide if they can accept a gift from a client?

(True) or False?

2.6 The AAT guidelines say that when preparing and reporting information members of the AAT should ensure that the information is presented: (tick one of the following)

	✔
fairly, honestly and in accordance with professional standards so that the information will be understood in context.	✔
simply and accurately and in line with international accounting standards so that a qualified accountant can understand it.	
briefly and concisely so that the key points are put across clearly to the user of the information.	

2.7 Syed, a newly qualified member of the AAT, has been offered a new job working for Clive. Clive has explained that from time to time the company raises invoices for some of its customers without charging VAT, provided they pay in cash. Which of the following should Syed do?

	✔
Accept the job and do as he is told by Clive as he is the boss and he will take responsibility.	
Explain to Clive that he is not prepared to accept the job unless all invoices are correctly accounted for.	✔

2.8 How should you complete the following statement?

When he/she has a problem resolving ethical conflicts a member of the AAT should…

	✔
consult the AAT Guidelines on Professional Ethics and make his/her decision based solely on this.	
take legal advice or contact the AAT Ethics Advice Line.	✔

2.9 Complete the following sentence:

Where a member is faced with an ethical conflict it is important that he/she keeps ....

	✔
quiet.	
written records.	✔

2.10 Pick out the four stages of the AAT cycle (as defined in the AAT CPD policy) from the following selection of words:

plan   assess   review   evaluate

record   action   improve   register

3 Confidentiality and taxation services

this chapter covers...

This chapter looks in more detail at the principle of confidentiality in relation to professional ethics and describes the ethical points relating to taxation work carried out by an accountant for a client or employer.

Specific areas covered include:

- *the accountant's duty of confidentiality in relation to the client's or employer's affairs*

- *the circumstances where confidential information can be disclosed*

- *the Data Protection Act and the way in which it affects members of the AAT*

- *ethical points relating to taxation services such as tax computations, completion of tax returns and giving of tax advice*

CONFIDENTIALITY

duty of confidentiality

One of the principles of professional ethics that we introduced in Chapter 1 is **confidentiality**. This means that information obtained during the course of an accountant's professional work should not be disclosed without proper and specific authority or unless there is a legal duty to do so. As this is such a fundamental principle of professional ethics, we will now look at this in more detail.

Members of the AAT have a 'duty of confidentiality' which means that they have **an obligation to respect the confidentiality of information about a client's or employer's affairs which has been gained during their employment or during the course of their professional work**. In addition to ensuring that they themselves observe this duty of confidentiality members must also make sure that any staff they supervise or manage also respect the principle of confidentiality.

We now give an example of a situation where a member must observe his/her duty of confidentiality.

example

a duty of confidentiality

Elliot Graves has been employed in the accounts department of Simons & Simons for a number of years and currently works as the Financial Accountant for the firm. On the train home from work on Friday evening he meets a friend and they start chatting. The conversation moves on to work and his friend asks Elliot how the job is going. He then goes on to ask how Simons & Simons are doing and specifically asks what kind of a financial year the company has had.

How should Elliot answer his friend's questions?

Elliot has a duty of confidentiality to his employers not to disclose any confidential information about the company that he works for. Elliot can answer his friend's first question as to whether his job is going well as this is a personal enquiry about Elliot himself. However, Elliot should explain to his friend that it is not appropriate for him to discuss confidential information about Simons & Simons financial results.

using confidential information

In addition to ensuring that they do not disclose confidential information, members of the AAT must ensure that they do not use, or appear to use, any information that they have access to for their own personal advantage or for the advantage of a third party.

We will now look in more detail at what this actually means. The point is illustrated in the following example.

example

a question of advice

Lubna Mirza is employed by a small firm of accountants and has been working on the year-end accounts of one of their largest clients, Richards Ltd. During the time that she spends at the client's premises Lubna learns that the company is currently in talks to take over another local company which is owned by a close friend of hers. The owner of Richards Ltd, James Richards, has mentioned that he would be willing to pay up to £250,000 for the firm, but only initially intends to offer £200,000.

Should Lubna tell her friend about James Richards' intentions? If not, would it be acceptable for her to give her friend advice about what offer to accept for her business?

Lubna has a duty of confidentiality to the client and so should not disclose any information she has obtained about Richards Ltd without specific authority from the company or unless she is legally obliged to do so. If she were to give her friend advice about what offer to accept, based on the information that she now knows, she would be using information that she had gained to benefit her friend (a third party), which is not acceptable.

Therefore, if Lubna's friend asks her for advice she should explain that Richards Ltd is one of her firm's clients and should suggest that the friend obtains independent specialist advice on how to value her business.

This example shows that an accountant must not use information for his/her personal advantage or for that of a third party.

We will now look at the second point regarding the use of confidential information. This is that members must not **appear** to use information that they have gained for their own personal advantage or that of a third party.

The point here is that even if the member is confident that he/she has not used confidential information for his/her own personal benefit or that of another, the member must also ensure that there is no possibility of anyone **thinking** that they have. It should not **appear** that the member has used confidential information inappropriately.

This is best illustrated with an example, using the same scenario as the last example.

example

the danger of 'appearing' to pass on confidential information

We will now return to the example of Lubna Mirza that we looked at above. If Lubna follows the course of action recommended in the example she can be confident that she has not used confidential information about Richards Ltd to benefit her friend.

Suppose that James Richards has completed the takeover of Lubna's friend's business and has paid £230,000 for it. If he were then to find out that the owner of the business he had bought was a close personal friend of Lubna's, he could quite legitimately question whether Lubna had passed on the information to her friend about what his maximum offer would be.

What could Lubna do/have done to ensure that her duty of confidentiality was not called into question?

As soon as she knew that James was intending to make an offer to buy her friend's business Lubna should have informed James of her relationship with the owner. She should also have explained to him that she is fully aware of her duty of confidentiality regarding information that she gains about a client and will not pass on any information. This would get her out of the dangerous situation where she could have 'appeared' to have advised the owner - simply because James would not have known otherwise.

the ongoing duty of confidentiality

We have already established that an accountant has an obligation to respect the confidentiality of information about employers or clients during the time that he/she is employed or is working for the client. This duty of confidentiality extends to the period **after the relationship has ended**.

In practice this means that any information that the accountant gains in the course of the professional work he/she carries out for a client remains confidential – even after the accountant is no longer employed by the client.

Similarly, information regarding an accountant's employer remains confidential even when the accountant moves to another employer.

DISCLOSURE OF CONFIDENTIAL INFORMATION

Having established that members have a duty of confidentiality, we will now look at the circumstances where confidential information can be disclosed. There are three main situations where it is acceptable to disclose confidential information. These are shown in the diagram below.

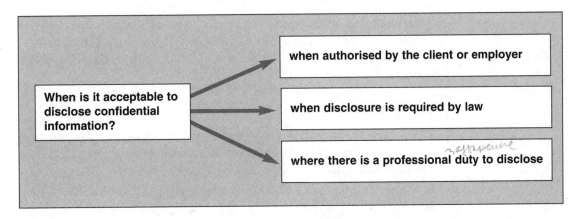

We will now look in more detail at these three situations.

authorised disclosure

In certain circumstances, the client or the employer may actually ask the accountant to disclose information that would otherwise have been treated as confidential.

The example that follows highlights a common situation where a client authorises the accountant to disclose confidential information to a third party.

example

authority to disclose

You work for a firm of accountants and receive a telephone call from a local builders' merchants asking for financial information about one of your clients who has requested to trade with them on credit.

How should you deal with this call?

Financial information regarding your client is confidential. Therefore you should not disclose any information about your client to the builders' merchants unless you have been authorised by the client to do so. You should contact your client to explain the situation and obtain specific authority to provide the financial information to the caller. Although verbal authority is acceptable, it would be better if this authority was given in writing.

When authority to disclose has been obtained from the client you can give the requested information to the builders' merchants. When doing this it is important to include a disclaimer making it clear that this is for the use of the builders' merchants only and is given purely to help them to make a decision about whether or not to supply goods on credit to your client. You should also explain that the information is given without any financial responsibility on the part of yourself or the firm for which you work.

This example illustrates that where a client has given permission, the accountant is then able to disclose confidential information. The main point here is that the accountant must get specific authority from the client before doing so.

disclosure required by law

In some circumstances the accountant will be faced with a legal requirement to disclose confidential information. This legal requirement to disclose confidential information can be divided into two main categories:

■ where the information is required as evidence in a court of law
■ where the law requires that information must be revealed to the relevant authorities in situations where the law has been broken

This is illustrated in the diagram below.

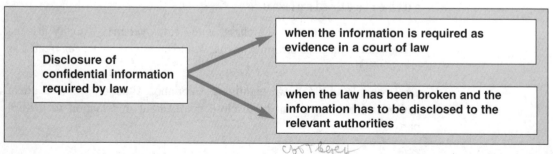

Disclosure of confidential information required by law

→ when the information is required as evidence in a court of law

→ when the law has been broken and the information has to be disclosed to the relevant authorities

We will now look at each of these two requirements in more detail.

evidence in court

There may be circumstances where an accountant is required to provide evidence in a legal case in court. The accountant may receive a witness summons from the court and be required to:

■ provide documents which will be used in court as evidence, and/or

■ to appear in court in person to give evidence

Alternatively the member might be the subject of a court order requiring him/her to disclose confidential information about the client.

In any of these circumstances the member has a legal obligation to comply with the request. As a consequence the accountant must break his/her duty of confidentiality to the client or employer, even if the client or employer has refused to give permission for the evidence to be provided. The power of the law, through the witness summons or court order, is stronger and will prevail here.

The following example illustrates this point in practice.

example

a legal question of confidentiality

Rachael Thomas acts as the accountant for Rolls Ltd. One of Rolls Ltd's suppliers has taken them to court for failure to pay for goods that have been supplied to them. There has been an ongoing dispute between Rolls and this supplier which has resulted in the non-payment by Rolls.

Rachael has been asked to provide copies of all documents relevant to this dispute, including invoices and correspondence, as evidence in the case. She has also been told that she may be required to appear in court as a witness to give evidence.

In these circumstances what steps should Rachael take before providing this information?

The information that Rachael has been asked to provide to the court is confidential. The first thing that she should do is to make her client, Rolls Ltd, aware that she expects to be called as a witness thereby giving them the opportunity to give her authority to provide the information in court. If they agree then she is free to provide the relevant documents or evidence as requested.

If, despite being informed of Rachael's likely appearance in court, Rolls Ltd refuses to give authority for her to disclose then Rachael must wait until she receives a witness summons. When this occurs she is legally required to comply with the summons and provide the relevant documentation, and if necessary, appear in court herself to give evidence.

disclosure where infringement of the law has occurred

Where a client or an employer has broken the law there may be a requirement for the accountant to disclose information to the relevant authorities that would otherwise be considered confidential.

A good example of this is in relation to money laundering.

A definition of money laundering is:

> **'to move illegally acquired cash through financial systems so that it appears to be legally acquired'.**

Basically, as the name 'money laundering' suggests, when the money has been gained through illegal activities it is seen as 'dirty money'. By using that money in legitimate trade or investment activities this is like 'washing' or 'laundering' the money so that it then appears to be 'clean' and legally obtained.

The current legislation relating to money laundering is the **Proceeds of Crime Act 2002,** the **Terrorism Act 2000,** and the **Money Laundering Regulations 2007**. It requires accountants to report immediately any suspicion that they have that money has been gained from illegal activities to the Serious Organised Crime Agency (SOCA).

Money laundering is covered in detail in Chapter 7. It is clear that in the circumstances described here the accountant has to disclose confidential information about a client if he/she considers that the client has broken the law. Disclosure in these circumstances should be made to the member's firm MLRO or to SOCA.

a professional duty to disclose

In certain circumstances, an accountant may have a **professional duty** to disclose confidential information. These circumstances are summarised below:

(i)   *to comply with the quality review of an IFAC (International Federation of Accountants) member body or other relevant professional body*

(ii) *to respond to an inquiry by the AAT or by a regulatory body of an ethical, investigatory or disciplinary nature*

(iii) *to protect the professional interests of the member in legal proceedings*

(iv) *to comply with technical standards and ethical requirements*

We will now look briefly at each of these four points. Taking the first point, if a member body of the IFAC such as the ICAEW decides to carry out a quality review then the AAT member is obliged to disclose confidential information to help with the review. Other member bodies of the IFAC include ACCA, CIPFA and CIMA. See page 150 for further details of the IFAC.

Secondly, in point (ii), a professional accountant must disclose confidential information if it is in response **to an inquiry by the AAT or by a regulatory body of an ethical, investigatory or disciplinary nature**. This inquiry could be in relation to the actions of the member in question, or an inquiry relating to an investigation into the actions of another member. If the member finds that in order to respond to the inquiry from the AAT he/she must disclose information that would otherwise have been seen as confidential, he/she has a professional duty to disclose this.

This type of situation could arise where the AAT has received a complaint from a client of one of its members regarding the fee that they have been charged for accounts work that the member has carried out. The AAT has a duty to investigate this complaint. In order to answer the questions that the AAT raises with him/her the member may have to disclose confidential client information to the AAT relating to the work that he/she has carried out.

Thirdly, in point (iii), an accountant has a professional duty to disclose if he/she is to protect his/her professional interests in legal proceedings. If, for example, an accountant was faced with legal action against him/her by a client, he/she would be permitted to disclose otherwise confidential information to protect his/her professional good name.

In point (iv) an accountant has a professional duty to disclose confidential information in order **to comply with technical standards and ethical requirements**. Technical standards in this case refer to International Accounting Standards (IASs), Standard Statements of Accounting Practice (SSAPs), Financial Reporting Standards (FRSs) and other relevant standards. Ethical requirements are those set out in the AAT Guidelines on Professional Ethics.

Deciding whether to disclose confidential information where there is a professional duty to disclose is a particularly difficult and complex area. Members are, therefore, specifically advised to seek professional advice before disclosing confidential information in these circumstances.

the decision to disclose

If a member makes the decision to disclose confidential information, there are three points which must be considered before making this disclosure. These points can be summarised as follows:

- The member must decide whether he/she knows all the facts regarding the issue and has enough evidence to back up these facts. If he/she does not have enough evidence then the member must use his/her professional judgement to decide to what extent (if any) the confidential information can be disclosed.

- Next, the member must decide who is the right person(s) to whom this information should be disclosed, and also how it should be communicated, for example by letter, report or verbally. This decision should ensure that the person provided with the information has the necessary authority to act upon it.

■ Finally, the member must consider whether he/she would face any legal consequences from disclosing confidential information, and if so how serious these consequences could be.

We can see that the AAT takes the subject of disclosure of confidential information very seriously and members must be very careful when deciding whether or not they should disclose.

In any circumstances where a member is unsure whether or not they should disclose confidential information, or where they are unclear as to how much they should disclose, they should consider taking legal advice from a solicitor or contact the AAT Ethics Advice Line. It is always better to get a second opinion if there is any doubt over the action that should be taken, rather than risk making the wrong decision.

DATA PROTECTION ACT

When a member in practice works for a client he/she will have access to a huge amount of information about the client. As we have discussed above, the member has a duty of confidentiality to the client regarding the disclosure of this information which is defined in the AAT Guidelines. In addition to this there are legal requirements set out in the Data Protection Act 1998.

The **Data Protection Act** gives individuals the right to know what information is held about them. It provides a framework to ensure that personal information is handled properly.

The Act works in two ways. Firstly, it states that anyone who processes personal information must comply with eight principles, which make sure that personal information is:

■ fairly and lawfully processed
■ processed for limited purposes
■ adequate, relevant and not excessive
■ accurate and up to date
■ not kept for longer than is necessary
■ processed in line with the individual's rights
■ secure
■ not transferred to other countries without adequate protection

The second area covered by the Act provides individuals with important rights, including the right to find out what personal information is held on computer and paper records about them.

Enforcement of the requirements of the Data Protection Act is carried out by the **Information Commissioner's Office** (ICO). Should an individual or organisation feel they are being denied access to personal information that they are entitled to, or feel their information has not been handled according to the eight principles, they can contact the ICO. Complaints are usually dealt with informally, but if this is not possible, enforcement action can be taken. Action taken by the ICO can range from issuing a 'stop now' order, to prosecuting those who commit an offence under the Data Protection Act.

notification

There is a statutory requirement for every organisation that processes personal information to notify the ICO. **Notification** is the process by which the person controlling the data gives the ICO details about the way in which the company processes data. Failure to notify the ICO could result in a fine if convicted. The next example illustrates this point.

example

Sonya is an AAT member who owns and runs a small accountancy practice with 12 employees. She has failed to notify the Information Commissioner of the way in which the practice processes data.

Sonya has committed a criminal offence under the Data Protection Act and consequently could be fined if convicted.

TAXATION SERVICES

One of the main professional services that members of the accountancy profession provide to their clients is taxation (tax) services. As you may know from your studies or experience, dealing with the tax affairs of an individual or a business can be very complex. Consequently many organisations rely on the professional expertise of accountants to deal with their tax. The AAT covers ethical issues relating to the provision of taxation services by its members in section 160 of the Guidelines.

Tax is a complex area and where detailed advice in this area is required, the AAT suggest that the member should telephone the AAT Ethics Advice Line.

ethics and taxation services

There are two main types of taxation:
- indirect taxation such as Value Added Tax (VAT)
- direct taxation including taxes on income, profits and other gains (eg capital gains)

The AAT guidance in Section 160 is general and applies to both direct and indirect taxes.

The key points have been summarised below, with the main principles illustrated in the example at the bottom of this page.

- When accountants are carrying out tax services for clients or employers they must ensure that they put forward the best case for the client without breaking the law or compromising their integrity or objectivity.

- Ultimate responsibility for the tax affairs of a client or employer remains with the client or employer and not with the accountant.

- An accountant should not be associated with a tax return if he/she believes that it contains false information or omits relevant information.

- If an accountant discovers a material error or omission in a previous tax return he/she should recommend that the client discloses this error to the relevant tax authorities immediately.

- If the client or employer decides not to disclose an error or omission the accountant should report the client's refusal and the facts surrounding it to the Money Laundering Reporting Officer under money laundering regulations without disclosing this to the client (for further details in money laundering see Chapter 7).

- If an accountant requires advice on detailed ethical issues he/she should contact the AAT Ethics Advice Line.

the importance of the Guidelines

Where accountants perform tax computations, complete tax returns and/or provide tax advice there are a number of ethical points to consider. Provided that they adhere to the guidance in section 160 of the Guidelines they will, in most cases, maintain the expected professional standards and will not compromise honesty and integrity when dealing with a client or an employee's tax matters. The following example highlights the main ethical points relating to tax.

---

example

a question of tax

A potential new tax client, John Sinclair, makes the following statement: 'The reason I chose your firm is because you saved my friend loads of tax and he didn't even have to check all the paperwork you gave him!'

What points should you raise with John in reply to this statement?

Your explanation should cover the following points:

- Although you will try to ensure that John pays no more tax than required, you cannot guarantee a reduction in the amount he pays, because all clients are different.

- Final responsibility for the accuracy of information in the tax return lies with John.

- John will be provided with a copy of the tax return and relevant calculations to check and can then ask any questions before it is submitted to the tax authorities.
- It is always possible that the tax authorities could challenge the information that is submitted.

Chapter Summary

- Accountants have an obligation to respect the confidentiality of information about a client's or employer's affairs acquired in the course of professional work.
- Accountants must ensure that any staff who work for them also follow the principle of confidentiality.
- Confidential information should not be used or appear to be used for the personal advantage of the member or a third party.
- The duty of confidentiality continues after the end of the relationship between the accountant and the employer or client.
- Confidential information can be disclosed when a client or employer authorises the disclosure.
- If the law specifically requires it confidential information about a client or employer can be disclosed.
- If an accountant has a professional duty to either comply with accounting standards, protect his/her professional interests in legal proceedings or respond to an AAT inquiry, confidential information may be disclosed.
- The Data Protection Act provides a framework to ensure personal information is handled properly.
- The person in an organisation that controls information has a duty to notify the Information Commissioner's Office of the organisation's process for handling data.
- When accountants are carrying out tax services for clients or employers they must ensure that they put forward the best case for the client without breaking the law or compromising their integrity or objectivity.
- Ultimate responsibility for the tax affairs of a client or employer remains with the client or employer and not with the accountant.
- An accountant should not be associated with a tax return if he/she believes that it contains false information or omits relevant information.
- If an accountant discovers a material error or omission in a previous tax return he/she should recommend that the client discloses this error to the relevant tax authorities immediately.
- If the client or employer decides not to disclose an error or omission in a tax return, the accountant should report them under money laundering regulations.
- If an accountant requires advice on detailed ethical issues he/she should contact the AAT Ethics Advice Line.

Key Terms	**duty of confidentiality**	the accountant's obligation to respect confidential information about the client or employer's affairs
	ongoing duty of confidentiality	the fact that the accountant's duty of confidentiality continues even after the end of the relationship between the accountant and the employer or client
	authorised disclosure	disclosure of confidential information by an accountant following authorisation by the client or employer
	disclosure required by law	the legal requirement for an accountant to disclose financial information about a client or an employer
	money laundering	to move illegally acquired cash through financial systems so that it appears to be legally acquired
	SOCA	Serious Organised Crime Agency
	Data Protection Act	legislation to ensure that data held about individuals is handled properly
	ICO	Information Commissioner's Office
	indirect taxation	a tax on goods and services such as Value Added Tax (VAT)
	direct taxation	a tax on an individual or company such as income tax and corporation tax
	tax return	an official form from HM Revenue & Customs on which an individual or company enters details of income and expenditure which are then used to assess a tax liability

Activities

3.1   The duty of confidentiality is only applicable to the member in charge of an assignment and does not apply to any staff working for him/her.

True or False?

3.2   When an accountant changes employer his/her duty of confidentiality to that employer ends.

True or False?

3.3   From the following list, select the three main situations where it is acceptable to disclose confidential information.

	✔
Where there is a professional duty to disclose.	✔
When the information is not finance related.	
When disclosure is required by law.	✔
When the member no longer works for a client.	
When authorised by the client or employer.	✔

3.4   Richard, a member in practice, has been asked by Juliette, one of his clients, to provide him with some financial information about another client who is a customer of Juliette's and who has not paid her for three months.

. Should Richard provide Juliette with any information about her customer?

Yes/No

3.5 Your client's bank has contacted you to get some financial information about your client. What should you do before supplying the bank with the information they require. Select one of the following suggestions.

	✔
Ask the bank exactly what they need and obtain a fax number to send it to them.	
Obtain written authorisation from the client to allow you to provide the bank with this information.	✓
Refuse to provide the information to the bank as it is confidential.	•
Ask the bank what they need the information for and then decide whether it is in the client's best interest to provide the information.	

3.6 Which one of the following is a valid definition of money laundering?

	✔
To move illegally acquired cash through financial systems so that it appears to be legally acquired.	✓
To process significant amounts of cash through a company's accounting systems without investigating its source.	
To use money acquired illegally to pay liabilities due to authorities such as HMRC.	
To finance illegal activities with illegally acquired cash without passing the cash through proper financial systems.	•

3.7 A member of the AAT has a professional duty to disclose confidential information to protect his/her .... interests in ....

Select the appropriate words from the selection below to fill the gaps in the sentence above.

personal **taxation affairs** **professional** •

organisation's **financial matters** **legal proceedings**

3.8 Which of the following is **not** one of the eight principles included in the Data Protection Act that must be complied with when holding personal information?

	✔
It is accurate and up to date.	
It is not kept for any longer than necessary.	
It is held securely.	
It is not kept for more than three months.	✔

3.9 What is the name of the process by which the person in an organisation who controls data informs the ICO about the way data is handled?

	✔
Registration	✔
Notification	
Subscription	

3.10 If a client or employer decides not to disclose an error or omission in their tax return, the accountant should report them to the Money Laundering Reporting Officer under money laundering regulations.

True or False?

this chapter covers...

This chapter focuses specifically on the ethical guidance that the AAT gives to its members who are employees – in industry, commerce, the public sector or in public practice. This chapter covers:

- conflict of loyalty to the employer and to the accounting profession
- whistleblowing
- the need for an accountant to support professional colleagues
- professional competence needed by an employed member
- operational risk
- inducements

INTRODUCTION

Much of the emphasis of the AAT Guidelines on Professional Ethics relates to guidance for members in practice – ie members who provide accounting and other services to clients on a self-employed basis. However, if you think about the qualified members of the AAT that you know, you will realise that probably the majority of them are employed in industry, commerce, the public sector, or in public practice.

There are three main ethical areas that are relevant to employed members:

- conflict of loyalties
- support for professional colleagues
- professional competence

We will now examine each of these in turn.

CONFLICT OF LOYALTIES

a definition of loyalty

One definition of loyalty is:

'being firm and not changing in your support for a person or an organisation, or in your belief in your principles'.

Society generally views loyalty as a good thing whether it is to friends, family or to employers. Employers are keen for their employees to be loyal to the organisation that they work for as this encourages stability within the workforce and a good team spirit, which in turn contributes to the success of the organisation. It also means that employees will be supportive of decisions taken by the organisation that they work for and will carry out the tasks that are expected of them.

One of the factors that will help to maintain an employee's loyalty to the organisation that he/she works for is a culture that encourages strong ethical values. We have seen in previous chapters just how important the AAT considers ethics to be for its members. But this need for strong ethical values is not limited to the accountancy profession. Every employee, regardless of their seniority in an organisation, should maintain an ethical approach to their work.

conflict of loyalties

Employed members of the AAT are expected to be loyal to their employer; but, as members of the AAT, they also owe a duty of loyalty to their profession. There is potential for conflict here. As an employee it would seem logical that the AAT member's first priority should be to support his or her organisation's objectives and the rules and procedures drawn up in support of them, provided that the organisation is acting in a legal and ethical way. However, there may be times when something that the employer expects the member to do conflicts with the member's professional and ethical values.

Because of the responsibility to his/her employer, a member may be put under pressure not to comply with the fundamental ethical principles. He or she may face pressure to:

- break the law
- breach the rules and standards of their profession
- be part of a plan for unethical or illegal earnings
- lie or mislead (including by keeping silent) auditors or regulators, or
- put their name to or otherwise be associated with a statement which materially misrepresents the facts

We can see that all of the above are very serious situations. Each one clearly conflicts with the ethical standards expected of a professional accountant.

Breaking the law is obviously not something anyone, never mind a professional accountant, should do. The rules and standards of the accounting professional are clearly there for a purpose and should not be broken by members of the profession. Note that breaching ethical standards includes not only active deception, but also a member misleading auditors by just keeping quiet when he/she knows the auditors have got something wrong.

So what happens if a member is put in a position where the employer puts pressure on him/her to do one (or more) of the above? Possible action that the member could take can be summarised as follows:

■ If the employer has broken the law, the member should try hard to persuade the employer not to continue with the unlawful activity and to rectify the situation as soon as possible.

■ If there is a difference of opinion between the member and the employer regarding an accounting or ethical matter, wherever possible this should be resolved with the involvement of more senior staff within the organisation. If necessary, the issue should be dealt with using the employer's formal dispute resolution process.

■ Where the issue between the employer and the member cannot be resolved and the member considers that he/she has exhausted all other possible alternatives then he/she may have no option but to offer to resign. In this case the employed member should explain to the employer the reasons for his/her resignation, and should at the same time maintain the duty of confidentiality to the employer.

It is worth noting here that the AAT strongly recommends that the member should obtain advice from the AAT or legal advice before taking the step of offering to resign. One important reason for this is that the law now protects an employee from dismissal for 'whistleblowing', ie breaking confidentiality (see next section). In other words, the employee should not have to be put in the position of having to lose his/her job when the matter is serious enough to be made public. Only the AAT or a lawyer (or both) can advise in this situation.

The process of dealing with conflicts of loyalty is summarised in the diagram opposite.

The area of conflict of loyalties and the ethical issues that it raises is illustrated in the example that follows.

example

a conflict of loyalties

Rona Hughes works as an accounts assistant in the accounts department of Peters & Son where one of her responsibilities is to prepare the quarterly VAT return for the company. It is now the end of the financial year and the Financial Controller has asked Rona to manipulate the figures to be included on the VAT return so that the company's year-end VAT liability is reduced.

This is clearly wrong and Rona should take no part in the Financial Controller's request to falsify the data that is to be included in the VAT return. But what should she do in these circumstances to resolve the problem?

As an employee of Peters & Son, Rona has a duty of loyalty to the company and to the Financial Controller as her line manager, but she also has a duty of loyalty to the accountancy profession.

In this case there is a conflict of loyalty between the two. In the first instance, Rona should explain to the Financial Controller that she has serious concerns about doing what he has asked and cannot be involved in such activities. If, at this point, the Financial Controller agrees with Rona that she is right, then no further action needs to be taken. However if, despite raising her concerns with him, there is still a disagreement, Rona would have to raise the issue with a higher level of management.

Finally, if Rona has no success when she raises the matter with the senior management of Peters & Son and the Financial Controller continues to falsify the VAT records, Rona will be faced with no alternative but to consider resigning. Before doing so she should take relevant legal advice.

If, after taking legal advice, she decides that resigning is the only course of action available to her, Rona should explain her reasons for resigning to the management at Peters & Son. She will still be bound by her duty of confidentiality to her employer and so should not tell anyone else these reasons at this stage.

If, on the other hand, her legal advisors consider that she will be able to keep her job and suggest that she 'whistleblows', she could do so (see next section).

dealing with conflicts of loyalty

LOYALTY CONFLICT PROBLEMS

the employer breaks the law

the member disagrees with the ethics of the employer

SOLUTIONS

persuade the employer to change to a legal way of doings things

persuade senior management to change internal practice within the organisation

REMEDIES IF SOLUTIONS DO NOT WORK

1 consider resignation

2 consult the AAT and take legal advice

3 offer to resign or 'whistleblow' if appropriate

the problems raised by conflict of loyalties

You will see that a number of issues are raised by the example of Rona Hughes above. Firstly, she has been put in a very difficult position as a result of the request made by the Financial Controller. He is more senior than she is and so has the authority to put pressure on her to comply with what he has asked her to do. Raising the issue with more senior management in the organisation is likely to cause a significant amount of tension between the Financial Controller and Rona, which could ultimately make her position within Peters & Son very difficult.

Resigning from the company would also be a huge step for Rona to take. The consequences of this could be that she may not receive a reference from Peters & Son, or may find it difficult to find another job.

With all these issues to contend with it is easy to see why some employees choose to remain silent about malpractices that occur within their organisation. They choose instead, to 'keep their heads down' and ignore the ethical issues that this raises.

whistleblowing

We saw from the section above and the example of Rona Hughes that the final option open to an employed member of the AAT when faced with a serious conflict of loyalties is to resign. In these circumstances the member continues to be bound by the duty of confidentiality that they have to their employer. However, some employed members may choose not to remain silent and may decide to 'blow the whistle' on the organisation that employs them where they have good reason to believe that illegal or unethical practices are occurring. In the case of Rona she may decide that she is not prepared to resign and 'go quietly'. Instead, after taking legal advice, she may decide to report Peters & Son to the relevant authorities.

So what do we mean by the term 'whistleblowing'? A whistleblower can be defined as:

> **'a person who tells someone in authority about something illegal that is happening within the organisation for which they work'.**

This can be a very serious step especially if the employee decides not to resign after blowing the whistle. In these circumstances the employer is unlikely to be very happy if one of its employees has reported them for something illegal and are unlikely to want the person to work for them any longer. Consequently is it important that the employee has some protection from dismissal if they choose to blow the whistle on the employer.

The Public Interest Disclosure Act, 1998 (PIDA) offers the employee such protection in certain circumstances. The PIDA (which is sometimes referred to as 'the Whistleblowers Charter') gives an employee protection where he/she discloses otherwise confidential information which he/she reasonably believes shows that one of the following has or is likely to occur:

■ a criminal offence

■ a breach of a legal obligation

■ a miscarriage of justice

■ endangerment of an individual's health and safety

■ environmental damage

In order to be protected from dismissal the employee must also be able to show that:

■ the disclosure is made in good faith

■ the employee reasonably believes that the information disclosed is true

■ the employee would otherwise be victimised or the evidence concealed or destroyed if the information is not disclosed

The Public Interest Disclosure Act, 1998 does make it easier for an employee to report an unethical or disreputable employer, but it still cannot offer complete protection from the employer who is the target of the whistleblowing. Recent cases of whistleblowing have resulted in employees being suspended pending an enquiry, or being dismissed at a later date for some unconnected reason. The main risk for an individual who has blown the whistle on an employer is the subsequent effect on future career prospects.

The following example highlights the serious consequences of deciding to 'blow the whistle' on an employer.

---

example

time to blow the whistle?

Stephanie Andrews works as an accountant for Harmsworthy Plc, a large quoted company. The Finance Director has asked her to help her with a scheme which she and the Managing Director have come up with. The directors have offered to pay Stephanie £5,000 for her help in the scheme which involves illegal dealing in shares of Harmsworthy. The Finance Director has made it clear to Stephanie that if she does not help them she will lose her job.

What should Stephanie do in this situation?

An employee cannot legitimately be required to break the law by his/her employer. In the first instance, Stephanie should raise her concerns with the directors of Harmsworthy and make every effort to persuade them not to break the law. However, this option could prove difficult for Stephanie as it is the senior management of Harmsworthy who are involved in the illegal activity.

Assuming Stephanie does not agree to break the law she is faced with two options. First, she could choose to resign from Harmsworthy stating her reasons for doing so. Secondly, she may decide to blow the whistle on the management of Harmsworthy and report them to the appropriate authorities. Under the second option she must be sure that the facts are correct and that she would be victimised and the evidence concealed or destroyed if she did not whistleblow.

This example highlights just how difficult it can be to make the decision to 'blow the whistle' and disclose confidential information about an employer.

For further reading, visit the AAT website (www.aat.org.uk) and read the article 'The Ethics of Whistleblowing' (use the word 'whistleblowing' in the site search facility to access it). This article summarises the main points that must be considered when deciding whether to contact the relevant authorities and whistleblow on an employer. The main points are summarised in the questions and answers in the table below.

SO WHAT DO I NEED TO THINK ABOUT BEFORE I WHISTLEBLOW?	
Q	**A**
Are you sure that you are fully aware of the facts and do you have some evidence to support the facts?	There is nothing worse than going down the whistleblowing route only to be told later that there was a reasonable explanation for something that you were concerned about.
Do you have internal procedures within the organisation that you have to follow to make a disclosure of malpractice?	If this is the case, you should consider using these procedures. Also, refer to the AAT Guidelines on Professional Ethics.
Have you explained the situation fully to management, ie your concerns and how the organisation could be affected by not addressing them?	Your explanations could help the organisation to understand the short-term and long-term implications of the problems you have highlighted.
Do you wish to obtain general and professional advice about what you are proposing to do?	It would be a good idea to contact bodies such as a trade union or the AAT.
Do you want to take legal advice?	Try a local Law Centre or Citizens Advice Bureau.
and last but not least . . . Have you thought fully about the consequences of blowing the whistle?	Your future career prospects may be in danger if you do not think the matter through and take appropriate advice.

This table shows that the decision to blow the whistle on an employer is a very serious step. Statistics show that whistleblowing is on the increase. Increasingly, employees are less likely to allow unethical and illegal practices to continue in the organisations for which they work. Accountants must ensure that they always promote best practice and by doing so encourage their colleagues to maintain high ethical standards.

SUPPORT OF PROFESSIONAL COLLEAGUES

supporting working relationships

In any job, employees are likely to have to work with other employees. Employed members of the AAT will most likely work within the accounting department of the organisation for which they work. Within this department there may be other qualified accountants, trainee accountants and members of staff who, although not qualified, will have a great deal of accounting experience.

The relationships between the members of an accounts team may depend on qualified accountants having seniority and therefore authority over other members, in other words the junior members of staff work for and report to a more senior qualified person.

One important aspect of these relationships is that the junior members of staff should have the opportunity to develop and make their own decisions on accounting matters. They should also be encouraged to form their own opinions on accounting matters even if ultimately these are found to be incorrect.

When dealing with more junior members of staff, members of the AAT should:

- allow other, more junior, members of staff to develop and use their own judgement in accounting matters
- deal with differences of opinion between themselves and other, more junior, colleagues in a professional way

The next two examples clearly highlight each of these points in practice.

example

a question of delegation

Stephen Boyd is the Senior Accountant for Brains Ltd, and is responsible for a team of 12 within the finance department of the company. He is more qualified than all of his staff both professionally and by experience, but despite the pressures of his job, he finds it difficult to delegate any of the more complex work to members of his team.

Rebecca Luebke is one of the assistant accountants in Stephen's team and has recently qualified as a member of the AAT. She is keen to put the skills that she has developed during her studies into practice and has asked Stephen if she could prepare the depreciation schedules for the year-end accounts. Fixed assets and depreciation is an area that Stephen always works on himself.

What should Stephen do in this situation?

Stephen is obviously uncomfortable delegating any of his responsibility to members of his team. But as an accountant he has a professional responsibility to allow colleagues to develop and use their own judgement in accounting matters. Therefore, Stephen should welcome Rebecca's enthusiasm to take on a new challenge and should allow her to carry out the work on depreciation. He should, however, ensure that he gives her adequate guidance on how the work should be performed.

When Rebecca has completed her work Stephen should ensure that he checks it and that he gives Rebecca constructive feedback on the work she has performed.

This example highlights the first key point made earlier regarding support for professional colleagues. AAT members should allow their colleagues to **develop and use their own judgement in accounting matters**. In the example above Rebecca will get a tremendous sense of achievement if she is allowed to carry out the work on depreciation and will have developed her own accounting skills at the same time.

The next example looks at the second key point on support for professional colleagues: dealing with differences in opinion in a professional manner.

example

a difference of opinion

Hugo Ross is the Financial Controller and Geraint Williams is a senior accountant in the accounts department of Henry Charles Ltd. Hugo is generally a very loud character and tends to shout at his staff and always gets his own way. At the end of the year Geraint has given Hugo a detailed schedule calculating the provision for bad debts which he has prepared.

Hugo marches into the office and shouts at Geraint that the calculation has been performed on a totally incorrect basis and that instead of being based on 5% of all debts over six months old it should be 3% of the whole debtor balance. When Geraint tries to reply Hugo tells him to 'shut up' and to change the figures on the revised basis he has indicated.

Has Hugo dealt with this situation correctly?

Hugo has completely dismissed Geraint's work without giving Geraint any opportunity to explain his calculations. This is not a professional way to deal with a colleague. Hugo should have taken Geraint into his office and asked him to explain the basis of his calculations. If Hugo still does not agree with Geraint, he should explain why he feels his basis for the calculation is more appropriate. If Hugo still considers that his method is more appropriate after discussing the issue in full he should then use his authority and state that his method of calculation should be used.

The important point to draw from this example is that accountants must ensure that they deal with differences of opinion in a professional manner and do not use a position of seniority to override the opinion of more junior staff.

PROFESSIONAL COMPETENCE

One of the fundamental ethical principles introduced in Chapter 1 was **professional competence and due care**.

There are a number of circumstances that will threaten the ability of a member in business to carry out work with the appropriate level of competence and due care. These include:

- if the member has insufficient time for properly performing or completing the relevant duties
- if the member has incomplete or inadequate information for carrying out the work properly
- if the member has insufficient experience, training and/or education
- if there are inadequate resources for example time, for the work to be carried out properly.

The significance of these threats will depend on the level of supervision and review that the member is getting at work. However, these threats must not be ignored and if the member decides that they are not insignificant then steps must be taken to reduce the threats to an acceptable level or to actually eliminate them completely.

Safeguards that may be considered by the member to reduce or eliminate threats include:

- obtaining additional advice or training
- ensuring that there is adequate time available for performing the relevant duties
- obtaining assistance from someone with the necessary expertise
- where appropriate consulting with a more senior member of staff, usually a manager at work, independent experts or a relevant professional body.

If even after doing this the threats cannot be eliminated or reduced to an acceptable level the member should consider whether to refuse to do the work. If the member does decide to refuse he/she should clearly tell the appropriate people.

It is clear that members are expected to take advice, assistance or training if they do not have the necessary skills to carry out an assignment or task that they have been asked to complete. In addition to this the member should not intentionally mislead an employer as to the level of expertise or experience he/she has, nor should a member in business fail to seek appropriate expert advice and assistance when required.

We will now explore what this means in more detail.

Many employees are ambitious and keen to progress within the organisation for which they work. Therefore, when there is an opportunity to do some more challenging work, this can be seen by employees as a way to show their ability and make a name for themselves. In this situation there can sometimes be a temptation for an employee to 'talk up' his/her experience and ability to perform the work in question in order to persuade the employer that he/she is the 'right person for the job'.

In the case of members of the AAT it is important that they should not exaggerate their own expertise or experience in relation to accounting skills. If an employed AAT member tells his/her employer that they have the necessary skills and expertise to carry out a particular task when they do not, this can have much more serious consequences.

This point is illustrated in the following example.

example

a question of experience

When Amit Odedra joined the accounts department of Warwick & Parks six months ago, he made it clear at his interview that he was very ambitious and keen to progress within the company. Mike Smith, the Finance Director, has noticed that Amit is very hard working and is regularly the last person to leave the office. He has therefore asked Amit to take on responsibility for preparing the monthly payroll for the company.

Amit has never done any payroll work before but would really like to take on the additional responsibility. What should Amit do in this situation?

Amit is very keen to progress within Warwick & Parks, but as a member of the AAT he should be aware that ethically he must not mislead his employer about the extent of his expertise and experience. Consequently, he should explain to Mike that whilst he is keen to take on the extra responsibility, he has no previous experience in payroll and so would need some training in this area before he could perform the additional work.

If Amit did not make Mike aware of this and took on the additional responsibility of payroll without any training, the implications for Warwick

& Parks could be very serious. Firstly, it is likely that the payroll would be incorrectly prepared which could mean (if the error was not picked up) that staff were paid the wrong amounts. Secondly, calculations of Pay As You Earn (PAYE) and National Insurance (NI) for payment to the Her Majesty's Revenue & Customs (HMRC) could be incorrect which could ultimately result in the company being fined.

We can see from this example that the fundamental principle of professional competence and due care is very relevant to the employed member. It would be ethically wrong for an employed member of the AAT to mislead the employer as to his/her expertise and experience. Errors could result which would have serious consequences for the employer.

OPERATIONAL RISK

An operational risk is a risk that arises from the way in which an organisation operates its business functions. It is a very broad concept which focuses on risks arising from the people, systems and processes and the ethical attitude of the organisation.

A widely used definition of operational risk is the one included in the Report by the Basel Committee on Banking Supervision. This definition is:

> **'the risk of loss resulting from inadequate or failed internal processes, people and systems or from external events'.**

It is important that the correct approach is taken to managing operational risks. Most organisations realise that nothing is perfect and completely free from risk. People make mistakes, processes will have imperfections and there are certain external factors that cannot be controlled. The key issue here is the size of the loss that a business is prepared to accept. Sometimes the cost of reducing or eliminating the risk is much higher than the cost of the loss that may be incurred.

Although failures in the systems and uncontrollable external factors affect operational risk it can also result from improper practice. If we take each of the factors that affect operational risk as defined by the Basel committee we can identify possible improper practices that could occur and the operational risks associated with them.

processes

Most organisations will have internal controls built into their systems and processes. For example most companies carry out a bank reconciliation on a regular basis to ensure that the cash book reflects what is actually held in the bank account once timing differences have been taken into account. If this control was not carried out the risk that money could be fraudulently taken from the business without detection is significantly increased.

people

When an organisation recruits new members of staff it is common practice to ask prospective employees to give names of references who the company can contact to confirm the individual's identity, qualifications and experience and also obtain opinions on his/her personality. If an organisation does not bother to take up references there is an increased risk that the people that it employs may not be competent and in the worst cases may not be honest.

systems

Most organisations are heavily dependent on computer systems in all aspects of their operations. Unless these systems have strong controls built in there are increased risks that the systems could be used to process fraudulent transactions. An example of this would be a payroll system. A lack of controls over access to the payroll system could result in fictitious employees being set up on the system and money being fraudulently paid to the person who set them up.

external events

In order to prevent unauthorised access to an organisations's computer systems the organisation must ensure that it takes adequate protection measures such as installing antivirus software and firewalls. Inadequate protection increases the risk that people could hack into the company's computer systems from outside, accessing confidential information or infecting the system with viruses.

INDUCEMENTS

In Chapter 2 we looked at the ethical issues for a member in practice surrounding accepting gifts and hospitality from a client. There is a similar issue for employed members of the AAT. An **inducement** is something that is offered to encourage or motivate a person to do something. Inducements may take various forms, including, gifts, hospitality, preferential treatment or even friendship!

Such inducements offered to an employed member could create a threat to his/her compliance with the fundamental ethical principles. The objectivity or confidentiality of a member can be threatened when an inducement is made in an attempt to:

- influence actions or decisions

- encourage the member to act dishonestly or illegally

- obtain confidential information

If a member is concerned that inducements could threaten his/her adherence to the fundamental principles he/she should assess the risks and decide what action should be taken. Options are:

- immediately inform higher management

- inform a third party of the offer, for example, a professional body such as the AAT (the member should consider taking legal advice before doing this)

- tell a close friend, colleague or relation if they are likely to benefit from the inducement and

- inform higher management in the organisation for which the person works

The following example illustrates the issues associated with inducements.

example

Uma is a member of the AAT who works as a management accountant for Pentagon limited. It is just before the company's accounting year end on 31st March. Her manager, Simeon, calls her into his office and explains that the company's results are not as good as he had hoped. As his bonus is based on achieving a certain level of profit he is quite concerned. He asks Uma to raise a number of fictitious invoices dated immediately before the year end to boost the sales and the profit figures for the year. He will then authorise credit notes to be raised against these invoices in the new financial year. In return for doing this Simeon says he will give Uma £1,000.

What should Uma do in this situation?

Simeon has offered Uma a financial inducement to do something dishonest. Uma has two options:

1 Uma could go to the Finance Director and tell him what Simeon has said, although there is a possibility that he may actually have asked Simeon to make the offer to her.

2 Uma could inform the AAT of the offer that Simeon has made. However, as this is a serious step to take, she may want to take legal advice before doing so.

■ Employed AAT members have a duty of loyalty to the organisation that employs them.

■ Employed members also have a duty of loyalty to the accounting profession.

■ Sometimes the loyalty to employer and the loyalty to profession may conflict.

■ Where an employed member believes that the employer is doing something illegal or unethical he/she should make every effort to persuade the employer to stop.

■ If the employer does not stop, the issue should be raised with more senior management or by using the employer's formal dispute resolution process.

■ If this does not resolve the issue, the member may have no alternative but to consider resigning.

■ Before resigning the AAT strongly recommend that an employed member should obtain advice from the AAT or legal advice.

■ Members may decide to whistleblow on their employers where they feel that serious malpractice is occurring.

■ Providing a member is acting in good faith when they 'blow the whistle' on an employer and so break the duty of confidentiality, he/she will be protected in many situations by the Public Interest Disclosure Act.

■ It is therefore recommended that members should consider taking legal advice before deciding to whistleblow on their organisation.

■ Members should always give support to their professional colleagues by allowing them to develop their own judgement on accounting matters and by dealing with differences of opinion in a professional way.

■ Employed members should not mislead their employers as to the degree of expertise or experience that they have.

■ Members should always seek expert advice, assistance or training where they do not have the necessary skills or experience to complete a task which they have been asked to carry out.

■ Operational risk arises from the way an organisation operates its business functions.

■ If a member is offered an inducement to influence his/her behaviour this may threaten the objectivity or confidentiality of the member.

■ If a member is concerned about being offered an inducement he/she should inform the appropriate person.

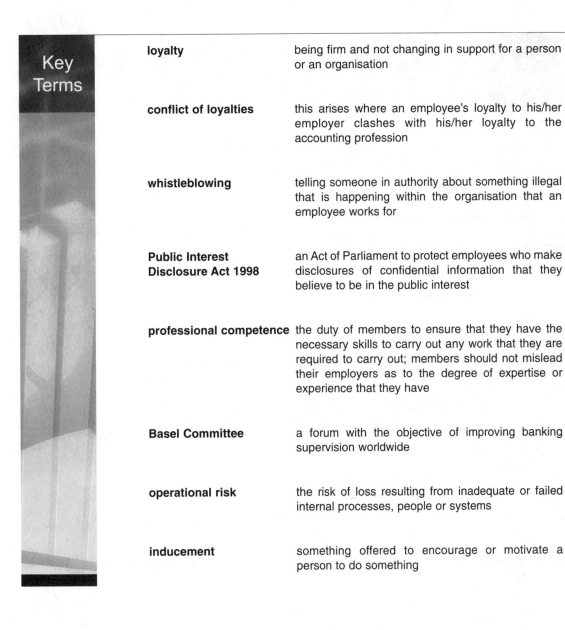

Key Terms	
loyalty	being firm and not changing in support for a person or an organisation
conflict of loyalties	this arises where an employee's loyalty to his/her employer clashes with his/her loyalty to the accounting profession
whistleblowing	telling someone in authority about something illegal that is happening within the organisation that an employee works for
Public Interest Disclosure Act 1998	an Act of Parliament to protect employees who make disclosures of confidential information that they believe to be in the public interest
professional competence	the duty of members to ensure that they have the necessary skills to carry out any work that they are required to carry out; members should not mislead their employers as to the degree of expertise or experience that they have
Basel Committee	a forum with the objective of improving banking supervision worldwide
operational risk	the risk of loss resulting from inadequate or failed internal processes, people or systems
inducement	something offered to encourage or motivate a person to do something

Activities

4.1 When a person who tells someone in authority about something illegal that is happening within the organisation for which they work this is known as (tick one option from the list below): ✔

professional competence and due care.	
professional indemnity.	
whistleblowing.	

4.2 The Whistleblowers Charter is another name for which of the following? ✔

The Money Laundering Regulations	
Terrorism Act 2000	
The Public Interest Disclosure Act 1998	

4.3 Which one of the following disclosures is not specifically covered by the Public Interest Disclosure Act? ✔

Professional negligence He Speak Kour	
Endangerment of an individual's health and safety	
Miscarriage of justice	
Environmental damage	

4.4   Sabrina, an AAT member, has been employed by Dandy plc for a number of years. Her manager, Ronald, has been paying the cleaning staff in cash without recording them on the payroll system. As this is illegal Sabrina wishes to make a protected disclosure to the directors of Dandy plc, but really does not want to lose her job.

What is Sabrina's position as a whistleblower in relation to the Public Interest Disclosure Act? Tick one option from the list below:

✔

She will not be protected by the act as this is not a qualifying disclosure.	
She will be protected as she has not told the AAT first.	
She will be protected provided she acts in good faith.	

4.5   Ralph, an AAT member in business, has been asked by his employer to undertake a major project for which Ralph does not have sufficient specific training or experience.

Complete the following sentence by selecting the appropriate option.

Ralph can still carry out the project if ....(tick one option from the list below):

✔

his employer makes sure that he has adequate support.	
he tells his employer that he does not have the expertise he needs.	

4.6   Complete the following sentence from the options below.

According to the Basel Committee on Banking Supervision, the definition of operational risk is:

'The risk of loss resulting from ....internal processes, people and systems or from external events.'

Tick one option from the list below:

✔

inadequate or failed	
a complete lack of	
very strong	

4.7 Failure to take up references before employing a new member of staff will reduce operational risk within an organisation.

True or False?

4.8 Offering someone a gift, money or preferential treatment in return for him/her doing something is known as which one of the following?

	✔
Whistleblowing	
Encitement	
Inducement	

4.9 Evelyn works for Tulip Ltd. She has been offered free use of the Managing Director's holiday home in Florida in return for ignoring the fact that he and his fellow directors regularly charge all their holiday flights through the business but do not pay the appropriate tax on these benefits.

Which one of the following courses of action should Evelyn follow?

	✔
Immediately inform the higher management within Tulip Ltd.	
Take legal advice and inform the AAT of the offer.	

for your notes

5 Independence of the member in practice

this chapter covers...

This chapter and the following two chapters of this book focus on the guidance on professional ethics given by the AAT to its members in practice – ie members who work for themselves or in firms, providing accountancy services to clients. This chapter covers:

- *the need for independence when carrying out assignments, and identifying threats to this independence*

- *assurance engagements*

- *situations where accountants act as agents for other organisations – eg for building societies*

- *situations where accountants are offered commission payments*

- *activities incompatible with the practice of public accountancy – running up gambling debts, for example*

- *dealing with assets held on behalf of clients, and assessing the possibility of fraud*

MEMBERS IN PRACTICE

The term 'members in practice' refers to members of the AAT who work for themselves providing accounting and/or accounting related services to clients. They can be 'one person' practices or partners in a firm. In both these cases they are strictly speaking 'self-employed' members.

what members in practice should do

AAT members who provide accounting, taxation or consultancy services in public practice must register on the AAT's scheme for members. They must also comply with the AAT Guidelines and Regulations for members in practice and the AAT's Guidelines on Professional Ethics.

what members in practice should not do

There are a number of functions that members of the AAT are **not** permitted to carry out. You are **not** expected to remember these, but they are listed briefly on the next page, as they are of interest:

- **external audit** (ie the audit of a UK limited company as required by the Companies Act or the audit of another body which requires the services of a registered auditor)
- undertake **investment business** or provide **corporate finance advice** to clients (ie activities subject to the Financial Services and Markets Act 2000)
- **insolvency work** (ie act as an insolvency practitioner in accordance with the provisions of the Insolvency Act 1986)

Members of the AAT **are**, however, permitted to work as part of a team providing these services, provided they are working for a suitably qualified accountant, eg ICAEW, ACCA.

assurance engagements

When an accountant carries out a statutory external audit he/she will give an opinion on the truth and fairness of the financial statements of the organisation that is being audited. An audit is known as an **assurance engagement**. This means that the accountant is giving the users of the report he/she produces a high level of assurance about the accuracy of the financial statements. In the case of an audit this is **positive** assurance. Note that, as we saw above, members of the AAT are not permitted to carry out an external audit of a UK limited company, but can be a member of an audit team.

There are also assurance engagements where an accountant gives **negative** assurance. This means that the level of assurance is not so high (moderate assurance). Examples of these types of assignments might be certifying grant claims, due diligence investigations or fraud investigations. In these cases the accountant is saying that he/she has found nothing that leads him/her to believe the information is wrong, rather than saying that everything is right.

AAT members are permitted to carry out negative assurance engagements and provide an opinion in these circumstances. You will find that some of the questions that you are faced with in the Professional Ethics Assessment will refer to assurance engagements; in these cases you need to remember that the AAT member will be giving an opinion on which the users of the information may rely.

INDEPENDENCE

the importance of independence

One of the fundamental principles that we looked at in Chapter 1 was **objectivity** which we then explored in more detail in Chapter 2 when we considered the need for an accountant to be independent both in mind and in appearance (see page 21).

Where a member is working on an assurance engagement there is a requirement that members of the assurance team be independent of the assurance client.

This independence must last for the whole of the period of the assurance engagement. This starts when the engagement begins and ends when the assurance report is issued. If the assurance engagement is of a recurring nature, the need for independence is on-going until the relationship is terminated.

The term independence may give the impression that the person, in this case the member, who is exercising professional judgement, is free from any relationship with the client, financial or otherwise. In practice this is impossible as every person in society will have relationships with others. The important thing is that the significance of these relationships must be considered.

The phrase that is used in the AAT Guidelines on Professional Ethics is:

> *'The significance of economic, financial and other relationships should also be evaluated in the light of what a reasonable and informed third party having knowledge of all relevant information would reasonably conclude to be unacceptable.'*

In simple terms if an unrelated person would think that the relationship between the client and the member is too close for the member to remain independent then the member must take further steps to distances him/herself.

The possible circumstances that could threaten independence are too numerous to detail. As we discussed in chapter one members of the AAT are expected to operate within a conceptual framework, rather than taking a rules based approach. This means that rather than complying with a defined set of rules the member must take the following approach:

- identify threats to independence
- evaluate whether these threats are clearly insignificant, ie deemed to be both trivial and inconsequential
- when the threats are not clearly insignificant address the threats by identifying and applying appropriate safeguards to eliminate or reduce the threats to an acceptable level

public interest

Some clients may be of significant **public interest** because of the type of business that they carry out, their size or their corporate status, or because they have a wide range of stakeholders. Such organisations include listed companies, companies that provide credit, insurance companies and pension funds. Stakeholders may include: shareholders, customers, supplier, banks and the general public.

The fact that these organisations impact on such a wide range of individuals means that there is a strong public interest in their financial statements. Consequently, members in practice, when they are working for this type of client, must pay particular attention to public interest when applying the conceptual framework to decide whether there are threats to their independence.

threats to independence

There are a number of potential threats to the independence of an AAT member in practice which are summarised in the diagram below.

In the text that follows we will look at each of these types of threat in turn and identify situations where a member could be faced with a potential problem with his/her independence and objectivity.

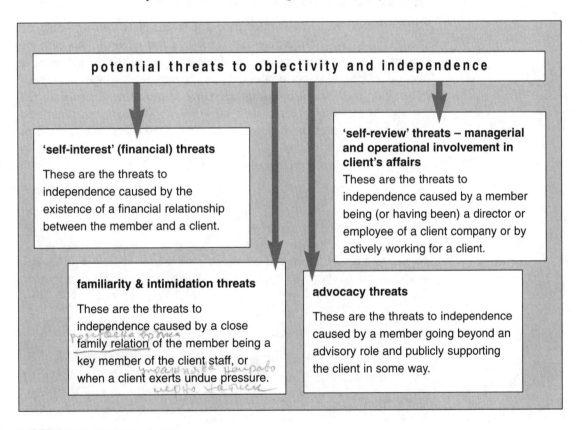

self-interest (financial) threats to independence

Where a member in practice has a financial involvement with a client or in the affairs of a client. This may threaten the objectivity of the member.

There are many examples of where the objectivity of a member may be threatened.

Set out below are four key areas where a financial involvement with a client can arise. They are:

■ direct or indirect financial interest in a client

■ loans to or from the client or any officer, director or principal shareholder of a client company

■ holding a financial interest in a joint venture with a client or employee(s) of a client

■ when the receipt of fees from a client or group of connected clients represents a large proportion of the total gross fees of a member or the practice as a whole

We will now explain these areas of financial involvement in more detail.

direct or indirect financial interest in a client

If the member is a shareholder in a client company he/she would be considered to have a direct financial interest in that client. In this case the member's independence would be threatened as he/she would have a financial interest in the performance of the client business which could affect his/her judgement when preparing accounts or providing financial or tax advice. This self-interest threat would also extend to shares in a client held by a close relative of the member; for example the member's husband or wife. The following example illustrates a situation of a self-interest threat resulting from a financial interest in a client.

example

shares in a client

Julie Parker acts as a self-employed accountant for a number of local firms. Her husband Simon and his business partner are considering buying shares in a local business and have been considering investing in one of Julie's clients, Doors & Windows Ltd. Simon discusses this proposal with Julie over dinner one evening.

What points should Julie raise with Simon?

If Simon and his partner were to buy shares in Doors & Windows this would create a self-interest threat to Julie's independence. The financial success of the company would have a direct impact on the value of the shares that Simon and his partner held. This in turn would affect the financial position of Julie and her husband.

Julie should explain to Simon that this would be a threat to her independence. In this situation Julie and Simon have two choices: either Simon can go ahead with his partner and buy the shares, in which case Julie should resign as accountant for Doors & Windows Ltd. Alternatively Simon should not go ahead with the planned purchase of shares in Doors & Windows Ltd.

loans to or from the client

If a client made a loan to a member who provided the client with accounting, taxation or other services, this could again affect the independence of the member. In this situation the client has financial influence over the member because of the money that is owed.

The example below illustrates a situation where this form of self-interest threat may arise.

example

loan from a client

Peter Moss is a member of the AAT and runs a small but successful accounting practice. Peter is keen to expand the firm, and during an informal chat with one of his clients, he explains that he is considering moving to larger premises and employing more staff. He also explains that he will need to arrange a substantial loan with the bank to allow him to do this. A few days later the client telephones Peter and states that he would be willing to lend Peter the money to finance his proposed business expansion.

Should Peter accept the offer?

Peter should not accept the offer of a loan from his client. This would immediately create a self-interest threat to Peter's independence through a financial involvement with the client. Peter should thank his client for the offer of the loan and politely say 'no, thanks'.

The only other solution would be for Peter to say to the client that he is no longer able to act as his accountant – but this is hardly realistic.

financial interest in a joint venture with the client

A self-interest threat would also arise for a member if he/she were to enter into a joint venture with a client or with an employee of the client. For reasons similar to those highlighted above, there would be a financial relationship between the client and the member which could compromise the independence of the member. We return to the example of the accountant Peter Moss to show how this threat could occur in practice.

example

the threat of a joint venture

A few days after Peter declined the loan from the client explained in the example above, he receives a further telephone call from the same client. The client says that he has been thinking about what Peter has said and believes he has a solution where he could help Peter with his business expansion without providing him with a loan. His suggestion is that he and Peter's firm embark on a joint venture to purchase the premises. Peter's firm would continue to provide accountancy services to existing and new clients. In return for his investment the client would expect a share of Peter's profits but would not be lending any money to Peter.

Should Peter now accept the offer given that the circumstances have changed?

Despite the changes in the nature of the offer, the client would still have a financial interest in Peter's firm and consequently there would be a self-interest threat to Peter's independence and so the offer should be politely refused. The only other solution, as before, is for Peter to resign as accountant for the client.

substantial fee income from a single client

If the fees that a member receives from an individual client represent a large percentage of the total gross fee income for the member (or the member's practice) this could again cause a self-interest threat to the member's independence. As the fee income from the client is so significant in relation to the member's total fee income this may well mean that the member cannot afford to lose the client which in turn could mean that the client has significant influence over the member.

example

the threat of substantial fee income

Sanjay Patel is a member of the AAT and runs a successful practice providing accountancy and taxation services to around 150 clients. His largest client, Emerson Ltd currently accounts for about 9% of his total fee income. Although Sanjay currently provides only accounting services to Emerson Ltd, the Managing Director of Emerson has asked whether he would like to take on the taxation work for the business. Sanjay estimates that the increased fees that this would generate would mean that Emerson Ltd would account for approximately 20% of his total fee income.

Should Sanjay provide the additional taxation services to Emerson Ltd?

The total fee income from Emerson Ltd if Sanjay were to take on the taxation work would represent a substantial proportion of Sanjay's total fee income. This could represent a self-interest threat to Sanjay's independence as Sanjay could become economically reliant on Emerson Ltd. Therefore in these circumstances Sanjay should not accept the additional work that Emerson is offering him.

self-review threats to independence

There is a threat to the independence of a member if a circumstance arises where he/she has to review his/her own work. This could be because the member used to work for the client and has now moved on to work for an accounting practice. Alternatively it could be because the member has moved from working for a practice into a role working for a client.

This type of threat to the independence of a member would also occur where the same situation applies to a close family member or colleague.

This self-review threat to independence is illustrated in the following example.

example

an insurmountable 'self-review' threat

Iris McDonald is a qualified member of the AAT. She worked for a number of years as Finance Manager for Catchett and Rank Ltd, a company that designs computer games.

After leaving the company Iris was employed as a senior manager by Michael Croft & Co, a local firm of accountants. A year after joining, Iris became a full partner in the firm.

Shortly after this she received a telephone call from a director of her previous employer, Catchett and Rank Ltd. He congratulated her on becoming a partner and explained that they were looking for some new tax advisors and thought that Michael Croft & Co might be a good choice.

Should Iris agree on behalf of Michael Croft & Co to accept the assignment?

Iris must use her professional judgement to decide whether it would be appropriate to accept the assignment. It would appear likely that in this circumstance she will have to review work that she has carried out and therefore there is a self-review threat. If it were possible for other members of staff at Michael Croft & Co to carry out the work so that Iris is not directly involved then it may be possible to reduce this self review threat to an acceptable level. However, Iris must consider how the situation would appear to a reasonable and informed third party and whether he/she would consider her actions to be acceptable.

providing other services for clients

There may also be a threat to independence where members provide **consultancy services** to clients – eg management consultancy and tax advice – they must take care that they:

- make recommendations
- do **not** make management decisions
- do **not** take responsibility for management decisions

They should also avoid reporting on management decisions which they have recommended. Members should be independent advisors and not managers.

familiarity threat to independence

Where a member of the AAT has a family relationship with the client or a key member of the client staff, this relationship may have a negative effect on the objectivity and the independence of the member. Because of a close or personal relationship a member may become too sympathetic to those person's interests.

The following example highlights a situation where such a relationship exists and the effect it could have on the independence of an accountant.

example

the threat of a family relationship

Liz Robinson is a member of the AAT who owns and runs a small firm of accountants together with her business partner Tom Crusoe. She shares a house with her sister Jo who runs a successful training company. Up until now Jo has managed her own financial affairs, but her business is rapidly expanding and she can no longer manage the books herself. In addition, she has recently taken out a substantial business loan from her bank and, as part of the agreement, they have requested regular independently prepared financial statements.

Jo asks Liz if she will take on her business as a client. Should Liz accept this assignment?

There is a close family relationship between the two sisters which is made even closer by the fact that they share a house together. This close family relationship constitutes a familiarity threat to Liz's independence; consequently Liz should not agree to Jo's request and should instead recommend an alternative accountant to her sister.

intimidation threat to independence

If an accountant takes on a client and a relationship develops in which the accountant is 'bullied' or put under pressure by the client – 'intimidated' in other words – then the independence of the accountant is under threat in a very real sense. As a result the accountant's reporting could be biased in favour of the client. In cases such as these, the accountant should be changed. If a larger firm is involved, a stronger personality could be brought into the accountancy team to counter the client's threat to its independence.

advocacy threat to independence

Advocacy means that you are seen to support the client's point of view publicly – even in a court of law.

In the context of a threat to the independence of a member the advocacy threat is that the member could go beyond the **advisory** role that he/she should take for the client and **actively speak** on the client's behalf or in support of the client.

By promoting the client's position or opinion too strongly this may mean the member's objectivity in the future may be compromised.

The threat that this situation could pose is illustrated in the following example.

---

example

an advocacy threat to independence

Hugh Davies is a qualified member of the AAT who provides a number of services to his clients, including accountancy services, management consultancy and taxation advice. Over the past few months Hugh has been providing management consultancy services to Naturally Green, a company that sells organic and environmentally friendly products.

The directors of Naturally Green are in the process of updating their marketing brochures and have asked Hugh to provide a written statement, as management consultant, endorsing the product range that they sell.

Should Hugh agree to provide the requested endorsement?

If Hugh were to provide an endorsement of Naturally Green's products he would be going beyond his advisory role for the client and would be 'taking a strongly proactive stance on the client's behalf'. This would have a seriously negative effect on Hugh's independence.

Consequently Hugh should refuse to provide the endorsement and should explain to the directors of Naturally Green the reasons for his refusal.

CONFLICT BETWEEN INTERESTS OF DIFFERENT CLIENTS

In Chapter 1 we discussed the issue of **conflict of interest** in relation to the objectivity of an accountant, explaining that members should not allow business or personal interests to prevent them from remaining objective and independent. The interests here are clearly those of the **accountant**.

Another situation where a conflict of interest can occur relates instead to the interests of the member's **clients**. Members who work in public practice normally have a significant number of different clients. Consequently there is a strong chance that at some point there may be a conflict of interest between two, or more, of these clients. For example the member may have a number of clients which work in the same market sector, all competing for the same customers, so the success of one client in increasing sales may well have a negative effect on another client in the same sector.

The issues for the member or practice working for clients where a potential conflict of interest exists are predominantly those of objectivity and confidentiality.

There are two potential problems which the member may face:

■ the member may provide services and give professional advice to one client where he/she knows that this will have an adverse affect on another of his/her clients (independence).

■ information gained about one client could potentially be beneficial to another and vice versa (confidentiality).

In many cases, the risk associated with these issues can be reduced to an acceptable level by compartmentalising the responsibilities and knowledge about each of the clients by using different members of staff to work on the client assignments. However, if this safeguard does not reduce the risk sufficiently then the member should not accept or continue one or more of the appointments.

When a member is considering taking on a new client or where there are any changes in the circumstances of existing clients the member should take all reasonable steps to find out whether a conflict of interests exists or could arise.

If a significant conflict of interest is identified between clients, the member should ensure that the clients involved are fully informed of the circumstances. This will then allow each of them to make an informed decision about whether to use the member's services.

The issue of conflict between the interests of different clients is illustrated in the example that follows.

example

a conflict of interest

Jim Kirk is an AAT member who runs Kirk & Co. a successful firm of accountants in Pineridge. Jim has recently been approached by Robert Redpool, one of the partners in Blackwell & Redpool, a local firm of builders asking if Kirk & Co. would be interested in carrying out some accounting and taxation work for them. One of Jim's existing clients, Bluebell & Whitelake is also a building firm located in Pineridge.

What points should Jim consider when deciding whether to accept the assignment for Blackwell & Redpool?

First, Jim must investigate whether there could be a conflict of interest between the potential client and his existing client, Bluebell & Whitelake. If he believes that there is, or could be, a conflict of interest between the two clients, Jim must then decide whether Kirk and Co have sufficient staff to use separate staff on each of the clients. This would reduce the risk that the interests of either client could be adversely affected if Kirk & Co took on the new work.

If Jim believes that he can adequately safeguard the interests of both clients he should then contact Blackwell & Redpool and Bluebell & Whitelake and fully explain the situation, including the staffing measures Kirk & Co intends to put in place. This will then allow the existing client and the potential client to decide for themselves whether they are happy to enter into, or continue in, a relationship with Kirk & Co.

If Jim decided that he could not sufficiently reduce the risks associated with the conflict of interest between the two builders, then he must either decline the appointment with Blackwell & Redpool (the more likely option) or end Kirk & Co.'s relationship with Bluebell & Whitelake.

SAFEGUARDS AGAINST THREATS TO INDEPENDENCE

How does a member in public practice ensure that his/her independence and objectivity are maintained when accepting or continuing to work for a client? How does a member deal with threats to that independence?

There are a number of possible safeguards and procedures that a member could put in place to help reduce the threats to a self-employed member's independence. These are in addition to any requirements provided for by law or by professional rules – for example the rules that govern the accountancy profession. A list of suggested safeguards is shown below. This list is not exhaustive, but it will help to summarise much of what has been explained in this chapter so far.

- the need for an educational and experience requirement (eg the AAT qualifications) for entry into the profession
- continued professional development (CPD) within the profession
- internal policies and procedures intended to promote quality control when dealing with clients and reporting on clients
- ongoing reviews of a firm's quality control systems
- arrangements to ensure that staff know about threats to independence and objectivity and can report any problems that relate to them
- a senior member of staff ('principal'), ideally a partner, who has not been involved in the day-to-day running of the assignment, should be actively involved, particularly in the final stage, to ensure that the objectivity of the firm is maintained
- consulting a third party such as a committee of independent directors, or a professional regulatory body (eg the AAT) in the case of any problems

■ separating the responsibilities on an assignment to help reduce the potential risks to independence that can sometimes arise – for example, ensuring that staff involved in preparing the accounts for a client are separate from those giving taxation advice will help to maintain the overall independence of the members involved

■ the threat to independence will be reduced if the senior members of staff involved in an assurance engagement are rotated (changed round) regularly, eg from year-to-year

■ in situations where external observers may believe that the independence of the firm could be compromised, the firm should consider making a public announcement, stating the way in which it will minimise this risk

■ if a firm cannot find any other way to sufficiently reduce or remove a potential threat to its independence then it should refuse to carry out the assignment involved

In this chapter we have looked at possible threats to independence and safeguards that reduce these threats to an acceptable level. Where safeguards are put in place to reduce threats to an acceptable level then the decision to continue with the assignment must be documented. This documentation should include a description of the threats that have been identified and the safeguards that have been applied to eliminate or reduce them to an acceptable level.

But what if it is not possible to eliminate or reduce the threats to an acceptable level? If the member feels that even after the safeguards are put in place the threats are still clearly not insignificant then the member must refuse to accept or continue working on the assurance engagement.

BUILDING SOCIETY AGENCIES

Until relatively recently it was fairly common in small towns in the UK for building societies to be represented by agents rather than opening full branches. These agencies were regularly operated by firms of accountants and allowed savers to deposit money into their building society accounts.

This has now become much less common since the Money Laundering Regulations and the Proceeds of Crime Act 2007 now require members to report any suspicions that they have to the Serious Organised Crime Agency. (Money laundering is covered in more detail in Chapter 7).

Because building society agencies predominantly accept deposits from personal customers, accountants are now faced with the risk of prosecution if they fail to investigate adequately the source of money that they accept from these customers.

In addition, members who are agents for a building society are only permitted to accept deposits. They are not allowed to provide any of the other services normally associated with a building society, including investments, insurance and mortgage advice, unless they are authorised under the Financial Services and Markets Act 2000. By displaying a building society sign and offering building society leaflets there is a real danger that the public may perceive that the accountant is actually offering some of these additional services.

Taking these points into consideration, in normal circumstances, it would be inappropriate for a member to act as an agent for a building society or other organisation.

COMMISSION

Sometimes a member of the AAT may receive commission or some other type of reward when he/she introduces a client to another organisation. For example, a member may receive an introductory fee from a bank or insurance company for introducing a client who subsequently opens an account or takes out an insurance policy. In these cases the client is in a position where he/she has trust and confidence in the accountant's advice – because sound advice is what he/she has come to expect. In such circumstances, the member will be accountable for the commission or reward to the client.

This means that where the role of the accountant involves representing the client or giving the client advice then the accountant must tell the client about the commission that he/she has been given for introducing them to another organisation. Under UK law the accountant is then obliged to pass over this commission or reward to the client, unless the client agrees that the member can keep it.

An example of where this could happen in practice now follows.

example

commission for an introduction

Jake Tweenie, a member in public practice, has been preparing the accounts for Big Sister Ltd for a number of years and has a very good working relationship with the directors of the company. With the increased exporting that Big Sister now undertakes, the directors have decided that the company should take out credit insurance on their debtors ledger. One of the directors has asked Jake to find a suitable insurer and arrange an introductory meeting.

After researching potential insurers Jake decides to recommend McCalls as a suitable insurer. When he contacts McCalls they explain that it is their policy to pay a commission to the introducer where a new policy is taken out.

What action must Jake take with regard to this commission payment?

If Big Sister decides to take out an insurance policy with McCalls, Jake must ensure that he fully discloses the introductory commission to the directors of Big Sister. He must also explain that he is legally obliged to pass over this commission to Big Sister whilst also pointing out that they can if they wish agree that he can keep it as a legitimate payment for the work that he has carried out.

INCOMPATIBLE ACTIVITIES

Most public accountancy practices will provide one, or more, of the following services to their clients:

- accounting
- auditing
- taxation
- management consultancy
- financial management

However, there may be situations where a member is also involved in another business, occupation or activity that may be unrelated to public accountancy services. In this case the accountant must ensure that this activity does not affect his/her ability to conduct professional business in accordance with the fundamental ethical principles of the accountancy profession.

The key point here is that a member of the AAT who works in public practice should not also be involved in any activity that will affect his/her integrity, objectivity or independence or will bring the good reputation of the accountancy profession into disrepute.

So what sort of activities would potentially fall into the category of 'incompatible activities'?

Here are some examples together with the reasons for their inclusion:

- a member who runs up significant gambling debts with a client organisation – the fact that the member owes the client money could impair his/her independence
- a member who consistently pays his/her own bills far beyond the due date – this could bring into question the integrity of the member
- a member who overcharges clients for the work that he/she performs –

again whilst this is not illegal it would be considered unethical and reflect badly on the member's integrity

■ a member who is generally sloppy in his/her work and does not take sufficient care over the assignments that he/she completes – this will reflect badly on the accounting profession and again questions the member's integrity

■ a member who is an active campaigner for animal rights, including being involved in demonstrations and potentially illegal activities – this may not be appropriate for the maintenance of the good reputation of the accounting profession

■ a member who represents an openly racist political party in local council elections – again this could bring the accounting profession into disrepute

A member of the AAT should be able to use his/her own professional judgement as to whether an activity that he/she is or potentially may become involved in could threaten his/her integrity or could bring the good reputation of the accountancy profession into disrepute. However, if the member has any doubt he/she should seek advice from the AAT using the AAT Ethics Advice Line.

CLIENT ASSETS

Members of the AAT who work in public practice may sometimes hold client assets; in many cases this is money that belongs to their clients. This could be as a result of a direct request from the client during the course of the services that they are providing to the client.

In all circumstances where an accountant is holding client assets there are strict rules and procedures that must be followed.

financial services and money laundering

There are a number of pieces of legislation that govern the holding of client assets by a member of the AAT working in public practice. First, under the terms of the **Financial Services and Markets Act 2000** members operating in the UK cannot hold clients' monies for investment business unless they have been authorised to do so. In reality it is unlikely that this would be something a member would actually become involved in.

Under the terms of the **Proceeds of Crime Act 2002** and the **Terrorism Act 2000** together with the Money Laundering Regulations a member should not hold client monies if there is reason to believe that they were obtained from, or are to be used for, illegal activities. If a member is not able to ascertain where the money has come from he/she should not hold the monies for the client.

fraud

One definition of **fraud** is 'an intentional deception made for personal gain or to damage another individual'. Fraud is particularly relevant to a member in practice if they are trusted by a client to hold assets for him/her.

The Fraud Act 2006 defines three classes of fraud:

- **fraud by false representation** – where a person makes any representation which they know to be misleading
- **fraud by failing to disclose information** – where a person fails to disclose any information to a third party which he/she has a legal duty to disclose
- **fraud by abuse of position** – where a person occupies a position where they are expected to safeguard the financial interest of another person, and abuses that position

The following example highlights the issues of fraud in relation to client assets.

example

Charles is an AAT member in practice who acts on behalf of a client, George, who is 89 years old. Charles has invoiced George for £4,800 for 'holding client monies', which simply involved being a signatory on George's bank account for a six week period. He has now transferred £6,000 to his own bank account from George's to settle the invoice and to cover late 'payment fees' of £1,200. When George's daughter, Alison, found out about this she complained to the police who are now investigating Charles for fraud.

Clearly £4,800 is far too much to charge for simply being a bank account signatory, and the additional £1,200 fees for later payment are inappropriate; regardless of the fact that there is no indication that the payment was late. Under the fraud act this will need to be investigated to see whether Charles has committed fraud by abusing his position as George's accountant.

procedures for holding client assets

When a member holds client assets this may pose a potential a threat to him/her complying with the fundamental ethical principles that we have already looked at. For example, there is a self-interest threat to a member's professional behaviour or even to their objectivity when a member is asked to look after money that belongs to the client.

To safeguard the member (and the client) against these threats there are a number of procedures that must be followed where a member holds money (or other assets) belonging to clients. These procedures are summarised below:

- client assets should be kept separately from personal assets or assets belonging to the firm

- client assets should only be used for the purpose for which they are intended

- a member in public practice should always be ready to account for the client assets, and any income, dividends, or other gains that have been earned, to any person entitled to such accounting

- a member should comply with all laws and regulations relevant to holding and accounting for client assets

The four bullet points above are included in the current ethical guidance from the AAT for holding client assets. However, historically, the guidance given to members who hold a client's money has been much more detailed. The list of points below is no longer included in the AAT Guidelines; however they are generally considered to be good practice:

- when opening a bank account for client monies a member should give written notice to the bank stating the title and nature of the account and requiring acknowledgement in writing from the bank that they accept the terms of the notice

- all client monies received by a member should be deposited without delay

- monies should only be withdrawn from a client account on the instructions of the client or for the client's benefit

- the client's account should never go overdrawn

- where the client's money is likely to remain in the account for a reasonable length of time and is a substantial sum of money, it should, with the agreement of the client, be placed in an interest-bearing account

- all interest earned on client monies should be credited to the client

- members should keep sufficient books and records clearly detailing how they have dealt with client monies both generally and in relation to specific clients

- a statement of account should be provided to clients at least once a year

The following example illustrates how these points would work in practice.

example

handling client monies

Emma Edgar runs a successful firm of accountants and tax advisors. As part of the tax services that Emma's firm provide they often hold money on deposit for their clients until the due date for payment of tax to HMRC. Although some firms will have only one account for client monies, it is this firm's policy to set up individual accounts for each client. Giles, a new member of staff, is unclear what to do when a new client asks him to hold £8,600 until the tax is due for payment.

What should Emma tell Giles to do?

Giles should first ascertain that the money has come from a legitimate source. Provided that he is satisfied, he must then write to the bank giving notice that an account should be set up in the client's name for the purpose of holding money for tax payments until the due date and requesting written acknowledgement of his request. If the money is likely to remain in the account for more than two months he should ensure that the bank pays interest on the balance.

When the account has been set up and the money paid in, Giles must ensure any further money is paid in without delay and that withdrawals are only made on instruction from the client. The account should also never go overdrawn. Clear and accurate books and records must be kept for the account and a statement provided to the client at least annually.

payment of fees

Can members use client monies that they hold to pay fees that they are owed? Basically, the answer is no. A member cannot decide to use money that they are holding for a client to pay themselves fees owed by the client – unless this has been specifically arranged with the client.

Chapter
Summary

- There are certain functions that members of the AAT are not permitted to undertake, these include external audits, investment business or advice and insolvency work.

- Members of the AAT are permitted to carry out negative assurance engagements.

- Members of the AAT who work in public practice must be independent both in fact and appearance.

- There are four main threats to the independence of a member working in public practice which are self-interest threats, self-review threats, familiarity threats and advocacy threats.

- There are a number of safeguards that members are able to put in place to minimise or negate these threats.

- Where a conflict of interest exists between two or more clients a member should take all possible steps to minimise the risks that could arise.

- Members who act as agents (eg as building society agents) should limit their duties to accepting client deposits unless authorised to do further activities under the Financial Services and Markets Act 2000.

- Where a member receives commission for introducing a client to another organisation he/she should give this to the client unless the client specifically says that the member can keep it.

- Members of the AAT should not engage in any business, occupation or activity which could impair their integrity, objectivity or independence, or which would bring the good reputation of the accountancy profession into disrepute.

- The Fraud Act 2006 defines three types of fraud: fraud by false representation, fraud by failing to disclose information and fraud by abuse of position.

- When holding client monies members should ensure that they have fully ascertained where the monies have come from.

- There are strict procedures that a member must follow when holding client monies.

Key Terms	**assurance engagement**	a professional engagement where the accountant gives an opinion that provides the users with some assurance on the subject of his/her report
	self-interest threat to independence	the threat caused by a financial relationship between the member and a client
	self-review threats to independence	the threat caused by a member currently or recently being a director or an employee of a client company or by actively working for a client
	familiarity threats to independence	the threat caused by a close family relation of the member being a key member of the client staff
	intimidation threats to independence	the threat caused by a client exerting undue pressure on a member
	advocacy threats to independence	the threat caused by a member going beyond an advisory role and publicly supporting the client in some way
	agencies	the situation where firms of accountants working in public practice operate as agents on behalf of building societies or other organisations
	commission	a financial payment made to a member for introducing a client to another organisation as a customer
	fraud	an intentional deception made for professional gain or to damage another individual
	client monies	money that belongs to a client and which the member is holding on the client's behalf while acting on the client's behalf

Activities

5.1   Which of the following is a member of the AAT not permitted to carry out? (Select all appropriate options).

	✔
preparation of financial statements	
statutory external audit	
investment business	✔
completion of tax returns	

½

5.2   Select the appropriate word from the choices below to complete the following sentence.

AAT members are required be to independent of............*all*............ clients.   ✗

assurance   **all**   **limited company**

5.3   Samantha is a member in practice. One of her largest assurance clients, Red News has recently merged with one of its large rivals and has asked Samantha to take on the new company as an assurance client. If she accepts this will mean that the combined fee income from this one client will be 40% of her total fee income.

Complete the following sentence by ticking the appropriate word in the table below.

This situation presents a potential .... threat to Samantha's independence.

	✔
intimidation	
self-interest	✔
familiarity	

5.4 Until recently Zoya, an AAT member who works for a large accounting practice has been seconded to the accounts department of one of her firm's clients. She is scheduled to work on the assurance team for that client.

What type of threat to independence does this pose? Tick the appropriate option.

	✔
Intimidation threat	
Advocacy threat	
Self-review threat	✔

5.5 Select the missing words from the selection below to complete the following sentence.

An advocacy threat to a member's independence may occur when a member... *promotes* ...a

client's ...*organisation*... to the point that his/her future ...*objectivity*... may be compromised.

business	**promotes**	**confidentiality**
objectivity	**organises**	**position**

5.6 (a) Vijay, a member in practice, performs accounting services for Brown Ltd and Blake Ltd. These two companies are in dispute over some goods supplied by Brown Ltd to Blake Ltd that they believe to be inferior quality.

Complete the following sentence by selecting the appropriate option from the table below.

For Vijay this situation threatens the fundamental ethical principles of…

	✔
confidentiality and professional behaviour	
integrity and objectivity	
objectivity and confidentiality	✔

(b) Which of the two options below should Vijay take?

	✔
Keep quiet to each of his two clients about his relationship with the other.	
Ensure each client is fully informed of the circumstances to allow them to make an informed decision.	✔

5.7   Which one of the following is not a safeguard against threats to a member's independence?

✔

rotation of staff involved in professional assignments	
consulting the AAT in the case of any problems	✓
a policy never to enter into an arrangement with a client who has any kind of business relation with an existing client	
continued professional development	

5.8   Jenifer, a member in practice, has received £500 commission for introducing one of her clients to a loan advisor. What should Jenifer do with this money? Select the correct option from the list below.

✔

Refuse to accept the commission.	
Keep the money and account for it as part of the fee for the assignment.	
Give the money to the client unless the client agrees that Jenifer should keep it.	✓
Send the money to the AAT and let them decide what to do with it.	

5.9   When considering incompatible activities for a member to be involved in which of the following statements is most accurate?

✔

Members of the AAT should not enter into any activities that they have not had authorised by the AAT.	
Members of the AAT should not enter into any activities that may bring the reputation of the AAT into disrepute.	✓

5.10 Charlie, a member in practice, has agreed to help one of his clients to fill out an application for a bank loan. Charlie knows that the client is currently having a bad year and is likely to have substantial cash flow issues later in the year. The loan application does not ask any questions about future cash flows so this has not been mentioned in the application.

Which offence under the Fraud Act 2006 is it most likely that Charlie has committed?

Select the appropriate option from the table below.

	✔
fraud by false representation	
fraud by failing to disclose information	✔

5.11 Graham, a member of the AAT, works as a sole practitioner. One of his clients, Rose, has asked Graham to hold on to £730 in cash for six weeks when it will be due to one of her suppliers.

Answer the following question by selecting the appropriate option.

What should Graham do?

	✔
Give Rose a written receipt and put it in his business's bank account.	
Inform Rose that under money laundering regulations he is not allowed to hold money on her behalf.	✔
Hold Rose's money separately from his personal money and the business's money.	

5.12 A member can decide to use client monies that they are holding to pay fees that he/she is owed?

True or False?

for your notes

6 Taking on new clients

this chapter covers...

This chapter looks at the principles members of the AAT in public practice should adhere to when they are taking on new clients.

This chapter covers:

- letters of engagement that are sent out to clients at the beginning of an assignment and which set out the responsibilities of the accountant and the client

- the ways in which fees and commissions are calculated for the work that is carried out for clients

- the procedures that should be followed when a client changes accountant

- the way in which accountants can advertise their services to obtain professional work

- the acceptable format for the names and letterheads of accountants in public practice

LETTERS OF ENGAGEMENT

purpose of the letter of engagement

When a member in practice is employed by a client to carry out any form of accounting work, either on a 'one-off' or ongoing basis, it is normal for the accountant to issue a **letter of engagement**. This is a formal letter which provides written confirmation of:

- the extent of the work that is to be undertaken by the accountant
- the respective responsibilities of the accountant and the client

The letter is agreed and signed by both the accountant and the client.

contents of the letter of engagement

There are several points that should be included in a letter of engagement that a member in practice sends to a client. A summary of these points is listed below:

- The letter of engagement should clearly set out the **nature and scope of the assignment**, ie whether it is accounting, taxation, consultancy or another type of service. Also if the member is going to produce a report at the end of the assignment, details should be given of the report's format.

- The letter of engagement should set out an appropriate **timetable** for the assignment, including when the work is due to start, how long it is expected to take and when reports are due to be made. It should also include whether the work is a one-off assignment or on a recurring basis.

- The letter of engagement should clearly set out the **responsibilities of the client**, for example the books and records that the accountant will need and when they will be needed.

- The letter should state that it is the **client's responsibility to detect errors and fraud**, unless, of course, the client and the accountant have agreed that this responsibility is a specific part of the assignment.

- The letter should contain details of how the accountant's **fees** are to be calculated, together with details of what action the accountant will take with regard to **unpaid fees**.

- The letter of engagement should set out who owns the **books and records** that are created during the assignment, ie the accountant's files that are created. It will also show details of the accountant's **policy on keeping, destroying and returning documents**. For example, the accountant may have a policy of returning documents to the client as soon as the bill is paid, or destroying documents after a set period of time if the client does not request them.

- If the accountant's work will be used by a **third party**, for example where the client uses the accounts to support a loan application, this must be specified in the letter of engagement and the accountants must make sure that they include a disclaimer that the information is provided only for client use and should not be shown to any other party without the accountants' prior consent

You should now study the sample letter of engagement which is shown in the Appendix (page 162).

FEES AND COMMISSIONS

providing a professional service

So far in this book we have discussed the ethical requirements that are expected of professional accountants and particularly AAT members. In other words, when carrying out work for their clients, members in public practice are expected to conform to technical accounting standards and to perform the work with integrity and objectivity.

Members of the accounting profession are able to carry out their work with these ethical requirements in mind because of the professional skills and knowledge that they have gained through their training and experience.

When accountants carry out assignments for their clients they are entitled to be paid for it – which comes as no surprise! We will now describe the ways in which accountants charge for the work that they do.

how fees are normally calculated

It is important when an accountant takes on an assignment for a client that both parties agree the basis on which the fees are going to be calculated. A summary of this should be set out in the letter of engagement.

Generally a member should base his/her fees on the following factors:
- the skills and knowledge needed for the work involved
- the level of training and experience needed
- the time that will be needed to carry out the assignment
- the level of responsibility that the work entails

In practice, this means that accountants normally base their fees on an agreed rate per hour, or per day, for the different levels of staff involved on an assignment. This is illustrated in the example that follows.

example

a question of fees

Briers & Bramble, a firm of accountants, has recently completed the year-end accounts for one of its clients, Penfold Ltd. Robert Briers has asked you to calculate the fees for this assignment and has provided you with the following information on the time taken:

- two Junior Trainees for eight days each
- one Senior for eight days

- one Manager for two days

- five hours of the Partner's time

Briers and Bramble's standard charge-out rates (excluding VAT) are as follows:

Junior Trainee	£175	per day
Senior	£280	per day
Manager	£500	per day
Partner	£120	per hour

How much should Penfold be charged?

The fees calculation for Penfold should be calculated by applying the standard charge-out rates to the number of hours or days that the assignment took at each level.

2 Junior Trainees for 8 days at £175/day		
= 2 x 8 x £175	=	£2,800
1 Senior for 8 days at £280/day		
= 8 x £280	=	£2,240
1 Manager for 2 days at £500/day		
= 2 x £500	=	£1,000
1 Partner for 5 hours at £120/hour		
= 5 x £120	=	£600
Total fees to be charged (excluding VAT)	=	£6,640

Note that in order to avoid any misunderstanding, it should be made clear whether the fees include or exclude VAT.

In the above example, the charge-out rates for different levels of staff increase as the seniority of the staff increases. This reflects the skills and knowledge and the experience of more senior staff and also the responsibility that they must take. The charge-out rate for a partner is the most expensive. This makes sense because the partner will be the most experienced member of staff and will take overall responsibility for the work that is carried out by his/her team.

quoting for new assignments

One of the key factors that will help a client decide whether or not to use a particular firm of accountants will be the fee that will be charged. It would be tempting for an accountant to provide a very low estimate for an assignment in order to improve the chances of getting the business. There is no reason why an accountant should not quote a lower fee than has been charged in a previous period provided it does not affect the quality of the work. However, it would be unethical for a member to quote an estimated fee, which he/she knows will substantially increase once the work is carried out, without telling the client.

The example that follows shows how this could arise in practice.

example

how low can you go?

Warne & Panesar, a firm of accountants, have been asked to produce a quote for a possible new client. During a meeting the potential client tells one of the partners, Kiran Panesar, that in order to be selected for the job the fee that Warne & Panesar quote must be at least 20% less than they are paying their current accountants.

Kiran knows that the client's current bill is £16,000 and that a 20% reduction would mean that the quote would have to be £12,800. She also knows that according to Warne and Panesar's standard charge-out rates the assignment should be charged at approximately £14,500. She is very keen to get the work and is considering what the implications would be if she were to quote for the work at the lower figure of £12,800.

What should Kiran do in this situation?

Warne & Panesar can quote a fee lower than the client is currently paying provided that the quality of the work that they carry out does not suffer. Kiran will need to examine the estimate that she has prepared to see whether it is possible to reduce it in any way. However, given the large difference between £14,500 and £12,800, this would probably mean reducing the number of hours or the grade of staff used. This could adversely affect the quality of the work.

Kiran could quote £12,800 as an estimate for the work and then increase the fee at a later date when the actual work is carried out. However, Section 5.6.4 of the Guidelines specifically states that this is not acceptable practice.

Therefore the only realistic options open to Kiran are either:

1   quote at the lower fee of £12,800 and accept that the firm will make a reduced profit on the assignment.

or . . .

2   quote her original estimate of £14,500 for the assignment, explaining that this is nearly 10% less than the client is currently paying and that the work cannot be carried out to the required standard for a lower fee than this.

contingent fees

Sometimes a client may ask an accountant to undertake work where the fee will be paid on a **contingent** basis.

Contingent fees mean that the client will only have to pay the accountant if the work results in an agreed outcome.

Contingent fees, where the fee is only paid if a specified result is obtained, cannot be charged on financial reporting services such as the preparation of a client's tax returns. This is because it could create a self-interest threat to the accountant's objectivity. For example the situation where the accountant will only be paid if the client's tax bill is below an agreed amount could influence him/her to adjust the figures to achieve this result.

Where an accountant is asked to perform a non-financial reporting service for a client on a contingency basis the member must think very carefully about whether there is a self-interest threat to his/her independence before agreeing to carry out the work on this basis.

In the following example, contingency fees could be charged.

example

contingent fees

Johann Pfaff is a member of the AAT who works in public practice. One of his clients, Septimus Ltd has asked him to prepare a business plan to support a loan application to the bank. The Managing Director of Septimus Ltd has asked that Johann's fee should be dependent on the success or otherwise in getting the loan.

Should Johann accept the assignment on this basis?

The MD of Septimus Ltd is suggesting that Johann performs this work on a contingent fee basis. If the loan application is not successful Johann will not be paid by Septimus for this work. Provided Septimus does not ask Johann to give a professional opinion on the business plan there is no financial reporting involved in this work. There is therefore no reason why Johann should not perform the work on this basis, provided he is happy to accept the risk in doing so.

percentage fees

An accountant will sometimes carry out work for a client where the fee is calculated on a percentage basis. For example, this could be as a percentage of money saved or money recovered in legal disputes. Sometimes, in these cases, the client will not be able to pay the accountant's fees unless there is a successful outcome to the work involved. For example, a client may ask his/her accountant to carry out some debt recovery work. If no money is recovered from the debtors then no fees will be due because any percentage of £0 is £0. Fees that are charged on a percentage basis will normally be treated as contingent fees.

The next example shows how a percentage fee could be agreed in practice.

example

percentage fees

Raymond Noir is an accountant in practice. One of his clients, Predator Ltd is keen to take over another business, Target Ltd (which is not one of Raymond's clients) and has been quoted a purchase price of £220,000. The management of Predator Ltd believes that this is too expensive and has asked Raymond to carry out some analysis to assist them in their negotiations to reduce the price. They have told Raymond that if he accepts the work they will pay him 30% of any savings they make on the initial price of £220,000, but only if the purchase goes through.

Should Raymond accept the assignment on this basis?

The work that Raymond has been asked to do is not financial reporting and he does not have to give a professional opinion. Therefore, he can accept this assignment on a contingent fees basis as there is no requirement for him to be independent and hence there is no self-interest threat.

expenses

Expenses such as travelling to and from the client that are incurred by the accountant because he/she is carrying out a particular assignment will normally be charged back to the client in addition to professional fees. Details of these expenses should be included in the letter of engagement.

the need for clarity in explaining the fees structure

Now that we have examined the various ways in which an accountant can charge for work carried out, you will be able to appreciate the importance of setting out **very clearly** in the letter of engagement the basis of the calculation of fees to avoid any misunderstanding.

CHANGES IN PROFESSIONAL APPOINTMENT

changing accountants

From time to time clients will decide to change their accountants. Possible reasons for this could be because they are unhappy with the service they are currently getting or that they believe that they can get a cheaper or a better service elsewhere. Also, in certain instances, it will be the accountant who decides to resign from an assignment with a particular client.

Regardless of whose decision it is, when there is a change in accountant, it is very important that the prospective accountant and the existing accountant communicate with each other promptly. This will allow the new accountant to check whether there are any professional reasons why he/she cannot accept the appointment.

Most practices would normally have a defined policy that its staff should follow when accepting new clients which should include the points covered in this section.

We will now describe the way in which this communication between 'old and new' accountants takes place.

communicating with the previous accountant

Communication between prospective and existing accountants should allow the new accountants to make a responsible decision whether or not to accept an appointment with a new client. At this stage it is worth pointing out that this decision is wholly that of the new accountant – the existing accountant cannot decide whether to give permission for the new accountant to act.

So how does the change-over actually work in practice?

First, the new accountant should check to ensure that the client has informed their existing accountant of the proposed change and has given them permission to co-operate with the new accountant.

The new accountant should then write to the previous accountant to request **professional clearance** together with any other relevant information he/she might need to take over the assignment. As the phrase suggests, if an accountant gives 'professional clearance', it means that there are no professional reasons why the new accountant should not take on the assignment for the client. Ideally this confirmation should be in writing.

It is the professional responsibility of the existing accountant, who receives a request from a new accountant, to co-operate fully and answer promptly. He/she should tell the new accountant whether there are any issues that his/her proposed successor should know about – or confirm that no such issues exist.

A sample text of a professional clearance letter is shown below.

the decision to accept a new appointment

When the new accountant has received a reply from the existing accountant he/she must then decide:

- whether to accept the appointment
- if the issues that the existing accountant has raised need to be investigated further before accepting the assignment
- whether to decline the assignment

There are a number of reasons why an accountant might decline an appointment, and he/she must use his/her professional judgement in individual cases. However, where an existing accountant's fees have not been paid by the client, this is not in itself a reason for the new accountant to refuse the assignment, although, of course, it could tip the balance towards a refusal of the assignment.

---

address

date

Dear Sirs

<u>Name of client</u>

We have been asked to act as accountant and tax advisor for the above client.

We are writing to enquire if you are aware of any professional reason why we should not take up this appointment.

If you are not aware of any reasons why we should not take up the appointment, we shall be grateful if you will kindly let us have the following information relating to the client:

1   accounts for the last financial year

2   trial balance for the last financial year

3   the most recent tax computations and tax return, as appropriate

4   any other information which would assist in the preparation of the accounts and tax computations

Yours faithfully

The next example highlights a situation where an accountant must decide whether or not to accept a new assignment.

example

accepting a new assignment

Mike Costas, an accountant who works in public practice, has been asked to act for a new client, Hexagon Homes. However, Hexagon Homes have specifically asked that he does not contact their existing accountants. They tell Mike that they will contact their existing accountants to obtain all the necessary information that he requires.

What should Mike do in this situation?

As part of the change in accountants for Hexagon Homes, Mike needs to obtain professional clearance from the existing accountants. The client's request not to contact the existing accountants means that this clearance cannot be obtained. Unless Mike can persuade Hexagon Homes to give permission for him to contact the existing accountant and for them to co-operate freely with him, then he should decline the assignment.

defamation клевета

Defamation means: **'to damage someone or someone's reputation by saying or writing bad things about them which are not true'.**

There may be circumstances where the information that an existing accountant communicates to the new accountant could be damaging to the client or other individuals associated with the client's business. Examples of this could include negative statements about the client's integrity or honesty, or may even relate to possible criminal acts carried out by the client.

Naturally, a client will not be happy if such information is passed on to the new accountant, particularly if they know that it is not true. In some cases this could lead the client to bring a legal action against the existing accountant for **defamation**.

If such a legal action is brought against an accountant he/she is likely to be protected by what is called '**qualified privilege**'. This means that the accountant should not have to pay damages to a client for defamatory statements provided the accountant has made these statements without deliberately wishing to harm or upset the client (ie maliciously). зло намерен

A statement made by an accountant will not be viewed as malicious provided that he/she honestly believes it to be true and has avoided making reckless allegations against a client which he/she has no reason to believe to be true.

This point is illustrated by the example which follows.

> ### example
>
> ### a question of defamation
>
> Jean Rook works in public practice and until recently has acted for a client Pawn & Castle. Jean has been concerned for a while about the fact that the directors of Pawn & Castle regularly take cash out of the business without accounting for it as drawings or salary. At a recent meeting there was a heated discussion between Jean and the Managing Director of Pawn & Castle which resulted in the client informing Jean that they intended to change accountants.
>
> Two weeks after the meeting Jean received a letter from another firm of accountants, Bishop & Co., asking for professional clearance. She replies stating the concerns she has about the cash withdrawals from the business and providing all other necessary information that Bishop & Co have requested.
>
> Three weeks later Jean receives notification of a legal action being brought against her by Pawn & Castle for defamation.
>
> Is it likely that Pawn & Castle's action for damages against Jean will be successful?
>
> Provided Jean can show that when she sent the letter of clearance to Bishop & Co she sincerely believed the statements she made were true, and there was no malicious intent, then it is unlikely that the action for damages by Pawn & Castle will be successful as Jean will be protected by 'qualified privilege'.

threats to fundamental principles

Before accepting a new client a member should consider whether this could cause any threats to compliance with the fundamental principles. For example the objectivity and professional behaviour of a member could be compromised if the member has a close or personal relationship with the owners or managers of the client. If a threat is identified then the member must consider what safeguards are in place to eliminate it or reduce it to an acceptable level. In this situation a detailed client engagement letter setting out the terms of the engagement should largely deal with these threats.

due diligence

In addition to assessing the threats to compliance with fundamental principles, before providing services to a client, members must consider whether their services could be used to facilitate money laundering or to finance terrorist activities. The Money Laundering Regulations 2007 apply to a member when the client and the member enter into a professional relationship which is likely to last for a period of time. If the member is going to act for the client in relation to transaction(s) amounting to 15,000 euros or more, then Money Laundering Regulations **must** be considered.

Where the above criteria are applicable the member must carry out sufficient **due diligenc**e. One definition of due diligence is:

> **'the process of evaluating a prospective business decision by investigating relevant financial, legal, and other important information about the other party'.**

Therefore, the member must have a detailed look at the client and the way it operates to decide whether he/she can enter into a professional relationship with the client confident that there are no ethical issues or any risk that they may be involved in money laundering.

The AAT Guidelines say that this due diligence should include:

- verifying the client's identity by looking at documents, data or other information obtained from a reliable source
- where the person who owns the business is not the person who runs it, the member should ensure that he/she fully understands the structure of the client. He/she should also carry out the same sort of verification of the identity of the owner
- the member should also find out what the client wants from the relationship

Where the member is unable to carry out adequate due diligence the member must decline the assignment. If, having carried out due diligence, the member has a suspicion that the client may be involved in money laundering or terrorist financing, the member must submit a report to the Money Laundering Reporting Officer or if the member is a sole practitioner the member must submit a Suspicious Activity Report to the Serious Organised Crime Agency (SOCA). It is the responsibility of the member to ensure that they are familiar with anti-money laundering and terrorist financing legislation.

The following example illustrates how due diligence would be carried out in practice.

example

Gill Gardener is a partner in Gardner & Shah, a firm of accountants. She has been approached by Mike McGann, the manager and co-owner of a small chain of local fish and chips shops, to act as his accountant. What does Gill have to do before she can enter into a professional relationship with Mike?

Gill must verify Mike's identity. The best way to do this is to ask Mike if she can see his passport, making sure that she fully explains to him why she needs to do this. She should also verify the identity of Mike's co-owner in the same way.

Finally, she should discuss with Mike exactly what he wants from the professional relationship with Gardner and Shah. In practice these discussions will probably take place during the negotiations between Gill and Mike and details will be included in the letter of engagement.

Provided Gill carries out sufficient due diligence and she is happy with the identity of Mike and his partner she can enter into a professional relationship with Mike.

additional related work

A member of the accounting profession may be asked by a client to take on some work that is separate from work that is already being provided by another accountant. An example of this would be where a client takes on one accountant to prepare tax returns and asks a different accountant to prepare the accounting statements.

In these circumstances the member being asked to carry out the additional work should inform the existing accountant of the work that he/she has been asked to take on.

The client may provide good reasons why the new accountant should not inform the existing accountant of his/her appointment. If the new accountant accepts the assignment without having communicated with the previous accountant, he/she must be aware of the increased risk of later finding out information which would have affected his/her decision at that time.

second opinions

Sometimes a member in practice may be asked to provide a second opinion on an accounting matter to a business that is not currently a client. This could cause ethical issues for the member. For example, if the member is not provided with sufficient information compared with the information that the original accountant had, this may affect his/her ability to act with professional competence and due care.

Where a member is asked to give a second opinion it would normally be sensible for the member to ask permission from the client to contact the existing accountant. If the client does not permit the member to do this the member should consider whether it is appropriate to provide an opinion.

OBTAINING PROFESSIONAL WORK

obtaining new work

There are a number of ways in which a member of the AAT working in public practice can obtain new work. They could be recommended by existing clients, by word of mouth or through advertising their services.

Members of the AAT must ensure that the way in which they advertise the services of their practice is consistent with the dignity of the accounting profession. This means the advertising should put across an image of a professional organisation that is committed to high ethical and technical standards.

legal and regulatory requirements on advertising

Any advertising must comply with the local law of the country where it takes place. In the UK it must also conform to the requirements of various advertising authorities including the British Code of Advertising Practice. This should particularly relate to legality, decency, clarity, honesty and truthfulness.

Accountants who are bound by the ethical code of conduct of their profession must ensure that they always comply with these legal and regulatory requirements.

advertising professional fees

One of the factors a new client will consider when deciding which accountant to use will be the fees that will have to be paid. It may, therefore, be tempting for the accountant to make his/her fees look as attractive as possible in advertising material.

It is very important for an accountant to be very clear as to how his/her fees will be calculated and exactly what services the fees will cover. Consequently, accountants will often offer a free initial consultation to potential clients at which fees levels can be discussed in more detail.

example

advertising fees

Jayne Reynolds works for Arthur Bowen & Co, a firm of accountants. She is currently producing an advertisement to put in the local evening newspaper to attract new clients to the firm. She shows the draft advertisement to several other members of staff who make the following suggestions regarding the section on fees:

'Why don't we offer a free no-obligation introductory consultation to all new clients?'

'Why don't we offer all new clients a 15% discount for the first year?'

Should Jayne include these suggestions in the advertisement?

There is no problem with Arthur Bowen & Co offering a free introductory consultation. This may appeal to potential clients as it will give them an opportunity to ask any questions they have and to clarify the fees that they will be charged.

The issue with offering a percentage discount is on what basis the 15% will be calculated. Jayne must make it clear that the 15% will be calculated on the fees that would otherwise have been charged by Arthur Bowen & Co for the service.

comparisons with other practices

Another technique that accountants might adopt when advertising professional services is to compare their practices with those of other accountants.

When a member or a practice chooses to make this kind of comparison in any of its promotional material, he/she must be totally unbiased and must be able to prove that what is being said is true. A member must take care not to make any negative comments about another practice.

Members must take particular care about any claims that they make about the size or quality of their firms because such claims are very difficult to prove. For example, it is impossible to know whether a claim to be 'the largest firm' in an area is a reference to the number of partners or staff, the number of offices or the amount of fee income. Similarly a claim to be 'the best firm' is subjective and cannot be supported by any facts. Therefore, statements like this should not be included in advertising for members' practices.

We will now return to the example of Jayne Reynolds (see previous page and above) who is preparing an advertisement for Arthur Bowen & Co.

example

comparison with other practices

The staff at Arthur Bowen & Co have made some other suggestions for points that could be included in the advertisement. Jayne is now considering whether or not to include any of them. These suggestions are:

'We're very good at what we do so shouldn't we say that we are the best firm in the area?'

'As we've got four offices couldn't we say that we're the biggest firm in the area?'

'All our clients say how reasonable our fees are, can't we say that we're cheaper than other firms?'

Should Jayne include any of these suggestions in the advertisement?

A claim to be the best firm in the area is subjective, and relies on personal opinions rather than on facts. It is therefore difficult to prove and so should not be included in the advertisement.

The number of offices that a firm has could be one measure of the size of a firm; however, size could also be measured by the number of staff or by total fee income. Therefore, again this claim should be avoided.

Finally, if in its advertising Arthur Bowen & Co says that it is cheaper than other accountants, the firm must ensure that the comparison is not misleading and relates to the same services provided by other practices. It must also ensure that the claim is based on fact and can be proved and also that it does not discredit or denigrate any other practice.

We can see that members must be very careful before deciding to compare their services with those of other practices in their advertising. They must ensure that any claims that they make can be proved and that they do not make negative comments about other accountants.

harassment

Members must remember that it is the client's decision whether to employ an accountant to act for him/her. We have seen in the above sections that it is acceptable for a member to promote his/her services through advertising. However, members must not promote themselves in a way that could be seen as harassment of potential clients. **Harassment** means **'behaviour that annoys or upsets someone'.**

An accountant must not put pressure on a client by repeatedly contacting them either in person, by telephone or in writing as this could be viewed as harassment. If the potential client were to make a complaint of harassment against a member of the AAT it would normally be up to the member to demonstrate that any repeated approaches he/she made did not amount to harassment.

This point is illustrated below with an example based on the example of Jayne Reynolds who is preparing an advertisement for Arthur Bowen & Co.

example

following up on client interest

The advertisement for Arthur Bowen & Co generated much interest in their services and Jayne has held introductory meetings with six potential new clients. She asks one of the junior accountants, Robert Crewe, to follow up these meetings with a telephone call to find out whether there is any further information that they may need.

On Friday morning Jayne comes into the office to hear Robert on the telephone, saying:

'Hello again! This is Robert Crewe from Arthur Bowen & Co. Hope you got my other messages. Please could you give me a call to discuss whether you would like our practice to carry out any work for you?'

What should Jayne do in this situation?

Jayne clearly intended that Robert make brief courtesy calls to these prospective clients. He has obviously made a number of calls to this particular potential client which could be viewed as harassment, especially as they have not called him back.

Jayne should now talk to Robert to find out how many times he has telephoned this prospective client and how many messages he has left. She should also ask him whether he has done the same with any of the other potential clients. Having done this she should telephone the prospective client(s) herself and explain that it was not her intention for Robert's calls to put pressure on them and they were merely courtesy calls to find out if they needed any further information.

Finally Jayne should explain to Robert the problems that his repeated telephone calls have caused and that he should not do this again in future as this could constitute harassment.

commission for introducing new clients

We have so far established that accountants are keen to attract new clients and will use a number of different techniques to achieve this aim. One of these techniques could be to offer commission to someone for introducing new clients to the accountant or practice. A member should only reward a third party for introducing a new client if the client is fully aware of this arrangement and the third party is a member of a professional body that complies with a strict ethical code comparable with the AAT Guidelines on Professional Ethics.

Given these requirements, it is unlikely that an accountant would have to pay a commission to a third party for introducing new clients. However, it is acceptable for an accounting practice to offer a commission to employees for introducing new clients to the practice.

The exception to this is where an employee moves from one practice to another and tries to bring his/her clients to the new practice. This is not considered professional behaviour and will create bad will between the two accounting practices. This is not generally considered to be ethical behaviour on the part of the accountant and should be avoided.

In the following example we will demonstrate how this could happen in practice.

---

example

paying commission for introducing new clients

Dominique Chapelle is a manager at Brown & Phips, a medium-sized accounting practice. She is keen to attract new clients and is trying to think of ways in which the firm can do this. So far she has come up with the following suggestions:

- offering a commission to all employees for any new clients introduced to the practice
- offering existing clients a discount on their fees for introducing new clients to the practice
- asking the practice's bank if they would be willing to introduce new clients to the practice in return for an introductory fee

Which of these suggestions is ethically acceptable?

There is no reason why Brown & Phips should not offer commission to its employees for introducing new clients to the practice, provided they are not clients of a practice for which the employee has recently worked.

When offering an existing client or the bank an incentive to introduce new clients, Brown & Phips must be very careful to ensure that the prospective client is aware of this arrangement and that the existing client or the bank are governed by appropriate ethical standards.

It is worth noting that most banks would not accept payment for introducing new clients to accounting practices, as this could be seen by third parties to compromise their independence.

PRACTICE NAMES AND LETTERHEADS

practice names

Most accountancy firms are named after past and/or present partners in the practice. For example the firm Osborne and Lynn will either currently have partners called Osborne and/or Lynn or will have had founding members with these names.

Some accountants, however, will choose to style their practices in a different way. It is important that the name that they choose is appropriate and dignified for a profession that has such high ethical and technical standards.

What this means is that when a practice is deciding what to call itself it should be careful that the name it chooses is not frivolous (silly), misleading, offensive or rude.

For example an accounting practice should not be called 'Sam's Tax Evaders', 'Super Cheap Accountants' or 'Men Only Accountants!'. In the case of 'Sam's Tax Evaders' this name could be misleading as it implies that the firm will help its clients to evade paying tax, which is illegal. The name 'Super Cheap Accountants' suggests that the practice will be charging very low fees for its services which are therefore likely to fall short of the high standards expected of the accounting profession. 'Men Only Accountants' could be seen as offensive as it suggests that the practice discriminates against women.

Two specific ways in which a practice name could be misleading are detailed below.

- A practice with a limited number of offices should not describe itself as 'international' merely on the grounds that one of them is overseas.

- It would be misleading if there was a real risk that the practice name could be confused with the name of another practice, even if the member(s) of the practice can justify the choice of the name.

There now follows an example of a situation where the name of a practice could be misleading.

example

what's in a name?

Toby Andrews and Michelle White are both members of the AAT and have decided to set up a practice together. They have decided that they will call the practice Andrews & White and are just about to register the name and get stationery printed. Toby is reading the local paper and sees an advertisement for Andrew White Accountants, a firm based in a town about 20 miles away.

Should Toby and Michelle go ahead and name their practice Andrews & White?

Toby and Michelle can, quite justifiably, lay claim to the name Andrews & White as it is simply both their surnames combined and follows the traditional custom of naming a practice after the principals. However, it would be easy for this to be confused with the other practice named

Andrew White Accountants which could mislead clients as to which firm they were employing.

Toby and Michelle then hit upon the idea of naming their practice White & Andrews Accountants, which would then get over the potential confusion over names.

A practice name must comply with partnership and company law as appropriate, and, in the UK, with the Business Names Act 1985. As part of your studies you are not expected to know this legislation in detail, but you should know that there are legal rules that restrict the name that an accountant chooses for his/her practice.

letterheads

Most organisations will have headed paper which they use for all their written communications. Accountants are no exception to this and will display their name and logos on all letterheads, documents and other stationery.

Letterheads should be of an acceptable professional standard, ie they should be clear, in good taste and consistent with the dignity of the profession. It is acceptable for the letterhead to include words such as Tax Advisers and Management Consultants provided the member(s) can show that they have expertise in that particular area.

Members are permitted to identify any specialist service that they provide in their letterhead provided they can demonstrate expertise in that particular area. They are, however, prohibited from using his/her designatory letters in the name of the practice. ie in the example above the practice can be called White & Andrews but **cannot** be called White & Andrews MAAT.

A typical suitable letterhead is shown on the next page.

Thomson & Rice

Chartered Certified Accountants

24 Abbey Chambers, Woolchester, WO7 6GF
Tel 01909 627323 Fax 01909 627333

ACCOUNTING SERVICES, TAXATION ADVISERS, MANAGEMENT CONSULTANTS

an accounting firm's letterhead

Chapter Summary

- A letter of engagement is sent to a client whenever an accountant is employed to act for a client.

- The letter of engagement should give details of the nature of the assignment, the timetable and the way in which the fees will be calculated. It should also show the respective responsibilities of the accountant and the client.

- Accountants are entitled to be paid for the work that they carry out.

- The fees that an accountant charges should be based on the skills and knowledge and the level of training and experience needed for the assignment, the time that the assignment will take and the level of responsibility that the work entails.

- Accountants' fees are normally based on an agreed rate per hour or day for different levels of staff involved in the work.

- An accountant can quote a fee that is lower than the client is currently paying provided that this does not affect the quality of the work and he/she does not intend to increase the fee once the work has been started.

- Fees can be charged on a contingent or a percentage basis provided they are not for a financial reporting assignment and do not create a self-interest threat to the accountant's independence.

- When clients choose to change their accountants it may be because they are unhappy with the service they are getting, or because they believe they can get a cheaper or better service elsewhere.

- When a client changes accountant the new accountant should check to ensure that the client has told the existing accountant of the change and has given them permission to co-operate with the new accountant.

- New accountants should request professional clearance from existing accountants before they accept an assignment for a new client.

- A statement made about a client in a professional clearance letter will not be viewed as malicious or defamatory provided the accountant honestly believes it to be true.

- Members should carry out due diligence before providing services to a client.

- When asked to provide a second opinion the member must ensure they are provided with sufficient information compared with the original accountant.

- When promoting their services, accountants should ensure that the advertisements are consistent with the dignity of the accounting profession.

- When an accounting practice is advertising its services it must comply with legal and regulatory requirements relating to advertising.

■ When referring to fees in advertising material an accountant must take care not to mislead potential clients as to the services to be provided or the basis of current and future fees.

■ Comparisons made in advertising with other accounting practices must be objective, relate to the same service, be factual and verifiable, and not discredit or denigrate the other practice.

■ Members must not promote themselves in a way that could be seen as harassment of potential clients.

■ Accountants will often pay commission to their employees for introducing new clients to the practice provided the employee is not 'poaching' these clients from a practice that he/she has previously worked for.

■ The custom is that most accounting practices are named after past and/or present partners in the practice.

■ When an accounting practice is deciding what to call itself it should choose a name that is consistent with the dignity of the accounting profession.

■ Accountants' letterheads must be of an acceptable professional standard and should be clear and in good taste.

■ Members should not use their designated letters in the name of the practice.

Key Terms

letter of engagement	written confirmation of the work to be undertaken by the accountant and the extent of his/her responsibilities and those of the client
professional clearance	a request for professional clearance is made by the new accountant to the existing accountant to ensure that there are no issues about the client that the new accountant should know about
contingent fees	fees that will only be paid if a specified result is obtained
defamation	to damage someone's reputation by saying or writing bad things about them which are not true
qualified privilege	an accountant should not have to pay damages to a client for defamatory statements provided the accountant made these statements without malice
harassment	annoying or upsetting a client by repeatedly contacting them
due diligence	evaluating prospective business decisions by investigating relevant financial, legal and other important information about the other party
SOCA	Serious Organised Crime Agency

Activities

6.1   Which one of the following is not normally included in a letter of engagement?

	✔
Details of how the accountant's fees will be calculated.	
Names of all the staff who will be working on the assignment.	
The nature and scope of the assignment.	
Details of the ownership of the books and records created during the assignment.	✓

6.2   One of the main purposes of the letter of engagement is to set out the respective responsibilities of the accountant and the client.

True or False?

6.3   Complete the following sentence with the appropriate word from the list below:

.... fees mean that the client will only pay the accountant if the work results in the agreed outcome.

supplementary   **percentage**   contingent

6.4   An accountant cannot accept a fee based on a percentage of any savings they make for the client.

True or False?

6.5 When accepting a new appointment the letter sent by an accountant to the client's previous accountant confirming that there are no reasons why he/she should not work for the client is called which of the following. Select one option from the list below.

	✔
Professional Clearance letter	✓
Management Representation letter	
Fees letter	
Letter of Engagement	

6.6 Select the option in the table below to which the following definition belongs:

'To damage someone or someone's reputation by saying or writing bad things about them which are not true.'

	✔
Conflict of interest	
Defamation	✓
Qualified privilege	

6.7 Zack, a member in practice, has been approached by Caroline Darcy to act as her accountant. What due diligence does Zack have to carry out before he can enter into a professional relationship with Caroline?

Select all the appropriate actions that apply from the list below.

	✔
Verify Caroline's identity	✓
Check that Caroline has enough money to pay him	
If Caroline has a business partner, verify his/her identity	✓
Notify the AAT of the relationship	

6.8   Select the missing words from the selection set out below to complete this sentence:

If a member chooses to compare his/her practice with other accountants he/she must be totally
.... and must be able to ....that what is being said is ....

[handwritten: true, unbiased ✓]   *[handwritten: prove ✓]*   *[handwritten: true ✓]*

biased	**true**	**prove**
understand	**unbiased**	**false**

6.9   A member should only reward someone for introducing a new client when which one of the following options occurs?

The client receives the same reward as the party who introduce him/her	
The client is fully aware of this arrangement	✓
The member informs the AAT of the arrangement	

6.10   Erica and Shibendra have set up in business together. Because Shibendra completes the accounts for his uncle in India the firm have decided to describe themselves in their practice name as international.

Which one of the following statements is true?

This is acceptable as the partners do carry out an international assignment	
This is misleading as they only have one overseas client	✓

6.11   Rhys, an AAT member in practice, has been accused of bringing the profession into disrepute when advertising his professional services.

This accusation is most likely to have arisen from which one of the following?

Stating in his advertising material that all his staff are fully qualified members of the AAT	✓
Promising to undercut any quote from another firm in the area by 30%	
Offering a free no obligation consultation to all prospective clients	

Legal considerations

This chapter considers some of the legal issues that an accountant in public practice may face when carrying out assignments for clients. It also covers the legal issues relating to money laundering which affect accountants in public practice and those who are employed in industry.

This chapter covers:

- *the legal position relating to the ownership of a client's books and records*

- *situations where an accountant can legitimately hold on to a client's documents until the client pays his/her fees*

- *how long an accountant must hold on to books, working papers and other documents before he/she can legally dispose of them*

- *situations where an accountant may be open to legal action and to pay damages to a client for failing to act with the necessary due care*

- *the responsibilities of accountants in relation to money laundering*

OWNERSHIP OF BOOKS AND RECORDS

what are books and records?

Anyone who works in an office will know that a huge amount of information is generated on a daily basis. This can be in various forms, for example paper documents, computer files, CDs and emails. When we refer to 'books and records' we are not simply talking about the paper documents, we include all of the above in this category.

legal considerations

In our normal everyday lives we would expect that if we create a document then it belongs to us or to the business for which we work. For example, if we write a report at work it is the property of the organisation for which we work.

There may, however, be circumstances where the decision as to who owns a document is not so clear-cut. For example, if you were to write a letter and send it to someone, does the letter belong to you or the person that you have sent it to? Or in the example of the report that you have written, if you are writing that report specifically for a client of your firm, does the report belong to you or to the client? These questions are less easy to answer.

When there is a legal relationship between a client and a professional person, such as an accountant, the rules on ownership of books and records are based on a combination of statute and case law.

Statute law is the law of the land, created by Parliament, whereas **case law** is law that has been established based on previous legal decisions in courts of law.

When a member enters into a contract with a client he/she must be fully aware of the legal principles that govern the contract. The member should also make sure that the respective rights and responsibilities of the member and the client are covered in the letter of engagement that they issue at the beginning of the assignment.

books and records – principal/agent relationship

As well as the requirements of the law, when deciding whether documents and records belong to the member or the client, the following points need to be considered:

- the type of contract (a legally binding agreement) between the member and the client (this is normally set out in the letter of engagement)
- the capacity in which the member acts for the client, ie whether the accountant is acting as an **agent** or not
- the purpose for which the documents exist or are created

Note that in law an '**agent**' is someone who acts for someone else, who is known as the '**principal**'. For example an estate **agent** sets up a house sale for a house buyer, a client who is therefore a **principal**.

The general rule relating to the accounting profession is that where a member acts as a principal – ie getting on with his/her own job – all documents that he/she creates during an assignment, such as notes and working papers, belong to the member.

The exception to this is the documents that the client specifically asks the member to create on their behalf, eg financial statements, which will belong to the client.

The two main types of work that a member performs for a client are accounting and taxation. We will now look at each of these and decide in each case who owns the documents and records.

accountancy work

If a member is preparing a client's financial statements, the working papers that the member produces during the assignment belong to the member and the financial statements that he/she creates belong to the client. If, however, the assignment is to create the accounting records for the client by entering the transactions in the client's ledgers then these accounting records also belong to the client. It all depends on what the client as 'principal' asks the accountant as 'agent' to do.

taxation work

When a member is carrying out taxation work for a client, such as preparing and submitting formal tax returns to HMRC, he/she is acting as the client's agent and therefore the documents completed will normally belong to the client.

If the member is providing tax advice to a client on request, then any written documents that he/she produces for the client will belong to the client. Any incidental working papers that the member produces will belong to the member.

correspondence

At the beginning of this chapter we questioned whether a letter that you send belongs to you or to the person who receives it. We will now look at the same situation where the correspondence is between a member and his/her client.

Under UK law, letters received by the member from the client, copies of letters from the member to the client and notes made by the member of discussions with the client belong to the member. Therefore, in most cases correspondence between a member and the client belongs to the member.

If, however, a third party becomes involved then ownership of the documents depends on the question of whether the member is acting as an agent ('person in the middle') for the client or not.

If a member is acting as an agent for the client, letters that the member receives from a third party and letters sent to the third party belong to the client. A good example of this is where a member is carrying out tax work for a client. In this case the member will normally be acting as an agent for the client and will be sending and receiving letters to and from HM Revenue & Customs. All letters that the member receives from the tax authorities belong to the client as the member is acting on the client's behalf. All copies of letters sent by the member to the tax authorities also belong to the client for the same reason.

This may all seem confusing, but can be summarised as follows:

- if the client has asked for a document to be produced as part of an assignment then this document will belong to the client
- if the member is acting as an agent on behalf of the client then the documents will belong to the client
- in all other cases the documents will belong to the member

The example that follows illustrates the question of who owns documents and records in different circumstances.

example

a question of ownership

Zahid Anwar is an accountant in public practice. For several years he has been working for a client, Maximus Ltd, preparing tax returns and producing the company's financial statements. He has just completed the financial statements for the current year and is having a final meeting with the Finance Director and the Finance Supervisor. Having presented them with the final version of the financial statements Zahid asks if there are any further questions.

The Finance Supervisor asks: 'When you did the tax return earlier in the year you gave us lots of documents, working papers and copies of letters. Why don't you give us all the working papers you produced when you were preparing the financial statements?'

What should Zahid tell her?

Zahid should explain that when he is preparing tax schedules and completing tax returns for Maximus Ltd, he is acting as the client's agent. In this situation all the documents and records that are produced belong to Maximus Ltd. When he is preparing the financial statements for the client these financial statements belong to Maximus Ltd, but Zahid's working papers belong to Zahid.

LIEN

A lien can be defined as: **'the right to retain possession of another's property until an obligation is paid'**. This means that a person can hold on to something that belongs to one of his/her debtors until the debt is paid. There are two types of lien, a **general lien** that gives the creditor the right to hold on to **any** of the debtor's goods, and a **particular lien** that relates only to goods that form part of a specific transaction between the two parties.

So why are liens relevant to accountants in public practice? When a member has carried out work on documents that belong to a client and the client has not paid the member, under UK law the member has a 'particular lien' over these documents. This means that the member is allowed to hold on to these documents and records until his/her fees are paid. For example a member may be working for a client preparing a draft income tax return for a client. If the client then refuses to pay the member's fees for this work he/she can hold on to the draft return until the fees are paid.

There are certain conditions that must exist in order for a member to have a right of lien, which can be summarised as follows:

- the documents that the member is holding on to must belong to the client and not to a third party

- the member must have obtained the documents by proper means

- the member must actually have carried out work on the documents and must have provided the client with a detailed fee note, and the fees must still remain outstanding for this work (ie not for past work)

---

example

a lien over documents and records

Holly Astley is a partner at Chance & Astley Accountants. One of the practice's clients, Collingwood Limited is refusing to pay the fee for tax work that Chance & Astley have carried out. The client says that the fees are higher than they were initially quoted. Holly has provided Collingwood Limited with a copy of the quote that clearly states the fees to be charged.

Chance and Astley have also prepared the personal income tax return for the Gerald Collingwood, the client's Managing Director, and have been paid for this work.

In these circumstances can Holly retain the tax documents relating to either Collingwood Limited or Gerald Collingwood until the fees are paid?

Chance & Astley have a particular lien over the tax documents that relate to Collingwood Limited because the practice has carried out work on them and has provided the client with a fee note for the work. Therefore Holly can quite legitimately hold on to these documents until the fee is paid.

Whilst it may be tempting for Holly to hold on to the documents that relate to the work done for Gerald Collingwood, Chance & Astley do not have a lien over these documents as the fees for this work have been paid and the documents belong to a third party. Therefore, Holly cannot retain the personal tax documents that belong to Gerald Collingwood.

There are some special rules that relate to the statutory books and accounting records of companies, and also where documents are claimed by an Administrator or Liquidator of a company. Further guidance on these matters can be obtained from the AAT or from a solicitor, but you do not need to know about these for your studies.

RETENTION OF DOCUMENTS AND RECORDS

why retain documents and records?

There is a general principle that once a certain amount of time has passed since an event has occurred, a legal action cannot be brought in relation to that event.

It is always possible that a client who is unhappy with work that has been carried out by his/her accountant may decide to bring some kind of legal action against the accountant. It is, therefore, important that the accountant holds on to all relevant documentation until enough time has passed that the client is no longer legally entitled to bring proceedings against him/her.

how long should documents be retained?

There are a number of laws in the UK that specify the periods of time within which legal action must be taken. If, however, there is no particular statute (law) that specifies time limits, the **Limitation Act 1980** sets out the default position.

The time limit for legal actions brought under simple contract law is six years. This means that a dissatisfied client could bring legal proceedings against his/her accountant any time up until the end of the six year period. It is, therefore, recommended that accountants in public practice actually retain books, working papers and other documents for seven years (ie an additional year to the six years) to allow a safety margin. Taxation records should be retained for seven years.

If a member is in any doubt about the length of time that documents and records should be retained it is important that they take legal advice from a solicitor.

PROFESSIONAL LIABILITY OF MEMBERS

a definition of liability

Liability means **'having legal responsibility for something with the possibility of having to pay damages'.**

Liability can arise from a number of causes, including criminal acts, breach of contract, breach of trust and negligent acts.

In law **negligence** is a breach of a duty of care that is implied in a particular situation or relationship. For example, a railway company has a duty of care for the safe transit of its passengers and an accountant has a duty of care to carry out assignments in a skilled and professional manner. If the railway company fails to observe safety measures (such as red signals) and the accountant makes mistakes in a tax return, they are both held to be negligent. We will now look at liability for professional negligence on the part of a member of the AAT. **Professional negligence** may occur if a client, to whom the member owes a duty to exercise reasonable care and skill, suffers a financial loss that can be proved is the fault of the member. Additionally, the member will have entered into a contract with the client, so this may be a breach of contract. An example of this is given opposite.

minimising the risk of professional negligence

For all assignments the following points should be covered to ensure that the possibility of a client suing a member for professional negligence is minimised:

- A member should ensure that before taking on an assignment the exact duties to be included (and equally as important, excluded) in the assignment are written down and agreed by both the member and the client. This would normally be done in the letter of engagement.

- If further duties are added to an assignment then the member should ensure that these are also written down and agreed by both parties.

- Where a member gives a client advice without having been provided with all the information he/she needs, the member must make sure that the client is aware of any limitations to this advice.

- If the member prepares unaudited accounts or financial statements for a client he/she must clearly mark on the documents that they are confidential and solely for the private use of the client.

- If a member is asked for a reference by a third party, (eg from a property company regarding the client's ability to pay rent) the member should state that this is an opinion and given without financial responsibility on the part of the member.

- If an assignment is very complex a member should take specialist advice or suggest that the client does so.

disclaimer of professional liability

When a member produces documents for a client, financial statements, for example, he/she may decide to attach a statement disclaiming professional liability. The exact wording of such a disclaimer will vary depending on the type of documents involved. The following is a good example:

'No responsibility for loss to any person acting or refraining from acting as a result of any material in this document can be accepted by X (insert the member's name or practice name). Professional advice should be taken before applying the contents of this document to your particular circumstances.'

It would seem that including a statement such as this is a simple and easy way for a member to cover him/herself and stop any possibility of legal action. However such a clause cannot be relied on in all circumstances and it is possible that a disclaimer may be seen by a court of law as an attempt by an accountant to escape his/her legal responsibility and therefore disregarded.

professional indemnity insurance

All members hope that they will never be put in the position where a client brings a legal case against them for professional negligence. However, it is possible that at some time this may happen. Members in practice should ensure that they have adequate **professional indemnity insurance**. This type of insurance is taken out by an accountant (or other professional) as cover against legal liability to compensate a third party (normally a client) who has sustained injury, loss or damage through a breach in the accountant's duty of care. Professional indemnity insurance is strongly recommended for student members who undertake self-employed work.

We will now look at an example where the issue of professional liability could arise.

example

a question of professional liability

Christopher Matthews works as an accountant in practice. He has recently received a request from the Managing Director of one of his clients to provide him with some personal advice on inheritance tax. Christopher has no experience in this area of taxation and has never given advice on inheritance tax before.

Christopher is considering reading up on this area of tax and taking on this assignment. However, he thinks it would be a good idea to make sure his professional indemnity insurance is up-to-date and to put a disclaimer of professional liability in the letter of engagement and in any documentation that he produces for the client.

Is this appropriate professional and ethical behaviour on Christopher's part?

If Christopher is unsure of his expertise regarding inheritance tax he should ensure that he gets the necessary advice and guidance from an appropriately qualified person. He should only take on the assignment if he considers that he has the professional and technical competence to carry out the work satisfactorily.

It would be unprofessional for Christopher to rely on a disclaimer of professional liability to cover the risk that he may not carry out the work properly. It is also unlikely that a court would allow him to rely on this should the client bring a legal action for damages against him were his advice to result in the client losing money.

All accountants should have professional indemnity insurance. But this should not be used as a 'safety net' in situations where an accountant does not have the necessary skills to carry out an assignment.

MONEY LAUNDERING

a definition of money laundering

In Chapter 3 we looked at the disclosure of confidential information where there has been an infringement of the law. The example we used for this was money laundering which was defined as:

'to move illegally acquired cash through financial systems so that it appears to be legally acquired'.

Put simply, this means using money gained illegally – eg through terrorist funding, drug dealing or other criminal activities – so that the money is 'laundered' or 'washed' and then appears to be 'clean' and legally obtained.

Guidance from Her Majesty's Revenue and Customs (HMRC) explains that money laundering takes many forms including:

- handling the proceeds of crime such as theft, fraud and tax evasion
- handling stolen goods
- being knowingly involved in any way with criminal or terrorist property
- entering into arrangements to facilitate laundering criminal or terrorist property
- investing the proceeds of crime into other financial products
- investing the proceeds of crime into the acquisition of property/assets

An AAT member will be guilty of a money laundering offence if he/she provides accountancy services while 'turning a blind eye' to the client's suspect dealings. This would be viewed as facilitating the client's illegal activities as detailed in the fourth point above. The value of the criminal property will have no bearing on whether or not a member should report a money laundering offence as there is no lower limit.

The example below illustrates a situation where a member has to consider money laundering.

---

example

Your client Eric has been given some company shares by his aunt, who bought them with money that she did not declare to the tax authorities (ie tax evasion). By accepting these shares is Eric guilty of money laundering? Are you as his accountant guilty of a money laundering offence?

The shares will only be criminal property as far as Eric is concerned if he knows or suspects that they had originally been acquired as a result of criminal conduct on the part of his aunt. He will then commit a money laundering offence if he deals in them. Conversely if he has no knowledge or suspicion regarding the funds that his aunt used to purchase the shares then he will not be committing an offence.

As his accountant you are in a similar position in that you will only be committing a money laundering offence if you know or suspect that the shares are criminal property. As Eric's accountant you can still be found guilty of money laundering if you knew about the criminal property even if Eric is innocent as your client's state of mind has no bearing on your obligations.

---

money laundering rules

The legislation and regulations relating to money laundering can be found in the following laws and regulations:

The Proceeds of Crime Act 2002 (POCA): this sets out the principal money laundering offence and the requirements to report suspicious transactions.

The Terrorism Act 2000 (TA): this sets out the principal terrorist financing offences and reporting obligations in similar terms to POCA.

The Money Laundering Regulations 2007 (the Regulations): these require sole traders and firms to establish procedures intended to detect and prevent activities relating to money laundering and terrorist financing.

money laundering penalties

Under the laws and regulations detailed above if an individual is found guilty of money laundering he/she, or the organisation that he/she works for, can be penalised. Dependent on the severity of the offence this could be an unlimited fine or it could be a prison sentence of up to fourteen years.

responsibilities for reporting money laundering

The combined effect of the **Proceeds of Crime Act 2002 (POCA)**, the **Terrorism Act 2000**, and the **Money Laundering Regulations 2007** means that where an accountant or practice has knowledge, suspicion, or reasonable grounds for suspicion that a client or an employer is involved with criminal property there is a legal requirement to report this to the Serious Organised Crime Agency (SOCA). Note also that if the member is working in an organisation which, due to its size, has appointed a Money Laundering Reporting Officer (MLRO), the matter should be reported to that Officer, who will then report to SOCA using a Suspicious Activity Report.

SOCA is interested to receive information about:

- the suspected person, such as, full name, address, telephone numbers, passport details, date of birth, account details
- the information on which the suspicion of money laundering is based
- details of the person making the report which will normally be the MLRO or sole practitioner.
- the whereabouts of the laundered property if it is known

One area where this must be considered is where, despite advice from his/her accountant, the client has failed to disclose an omission or error in his/her tax affairs. Although it would seem logical to report this to HMRC, a member should report this to the firm's MLRO or if he/she is a sole practitioner, to SOCA.

If a member believes that a fraud had been committed then he/she also has a duty to report this to the police.

Practices and employers must also have training and internal procedures in place to ensure that they comply with the reporting requirements above. If these procedures are not in place the accountant may be liable for a fine or imprisonment or both.

Clearly this an important legal issue that the accounting profession takes very seriously. Members and student members must ensure that they are familiar with their employer's internal procedures for reporting suspicions of money laundering. Employers must ensure that all their staff have been provided with adequate training on their legal obligations in respect of money laundering and the firms anti-money laundering procedures.

failure to report

We have already discussed the requirement for a member to report his/her suspicion of money laundering to the firm's MLRO or directly to SOCA. However, it is worth noting that it is an offence of **'failure to report'** under the POCA if a member does not report his/her suspicion. This offence carries a maximum penalty of five years imprisonment and/or a fine.

tipping off

POCA has created a criminal offence of **'tipping off'**. This is where someone who knows, or thinks they know that, a report of money laundering has been made to SOCA warns (or 'tips off') the person(s) suspected. Where this happens the person who 'tips off' the suspect is liable to be prosecuted as well as the person who is carrying out the money laundering.

An accountant who discovers that an employer or a client is potentially money laundering must report his/her suspicions to the Money Laundering Reporting Officer or SOCA. They must ensure, however, that they do not make the employer or client aware of this as this would be considered tipping off.

Although tipping off is an offence, an accountant is entitled to advise his/her clients in general terms about the issue of money laundering.

The following example illustrates the serious implications of money laundering.

example

a case of money laundering

Wilfred Joyce is an accountant in public practice. One of his clients is an antiques dealer called Louis Kans. One Friday Wilfred receives a telephone enquiry from Louis, who says that a customer is in the shop asking to buy a piece of furniture for £11,000. The customer is offering to pay Louis in cash.

What should Wilfred advise in this situation?

Louis has been offered a large amount of cash but does not really know where it has come from. Although the customer may have good reasons for having such a large amount of cash there is a risk that it may not have been gained through legal means.

As Wilfred's objective in this situation is to ensure that his client does not breach the Money Laundering Regulations 2007, he should advise Louis to identify the customer and verify the source of the cash before accepting it, thus satisfying himself that the cash is not the proceeds of some crime.

If despite Wilfred's advice Louis then goes on and deals with the customer on a cash basis then Wilfred will have no option but to report him to SOCA.

accepting new clients

In Chapter 6 we described the methods accountants use to obtain new clients. There may, however, be occasions where an accountant is not able to take on a new client. This could be because the accountant does not have sufficient staff with the appropriate expertise to carry out the work for the client. Or it could simply be that the accountant does not feel that it is appropriate to take on the client. One of the reasons for this could relate to money laundering.

The Money Laundering Regulations 2007 require that as soon as it is reasonably practicable, accountants should obtain satisfactory evidence of the identity of a new client. The most common way of doing this is for the accountant to ask to see the client's passport or driving licence and a current utility bill showing the client's name and address.

Where the client is a business rather than an individual the accountant will not need to obtain evidence of the identity of all individuals involved in the business. Normally only the principal contacts and the people who control the business should be identified.

Chapter Summary

- The rules on ownership of books and records are mainly based on a combination of statute law and case law.

- If a client asks for a document to be produced as part of an assignment then this document will belong to the client.

- If an accountant is acting as an agent on behalf of a client (for example when performing tax work) then the documents will belong to the client.

- If a client fails to pay an accountant for work that he/she has performed, the accountant has a particular lien over the client's books and records and can hold on to them until the fees are paid.

- There are a number of laws in the UK that specify the length of time within which legal action must be taken.

- Accountants should ideally retain books, working paper and other documents for seven years before disposing of them (the law implies a requirement of a period of six years).

- Taxation records should be kept for seven years.

- Accountants have a professional duty of care when carrying out work for clients and have professional liability for the work that they carry out.

- Where a client suffers a loss as a result of work carried out by an accountant they may bring a legal action against the accountant for professional negligence.

- Accountants will sometimes include a disclaimer of professional liability in documents that they produce for clients in an attempt to minimise the risk of a case of professional negligence being brought against them.

- Members of the AAT should have sufficient professional indemnity insurance to cover against legal liability to compensate a client who has sustained loss through a breach of the accountant's duty of care.

- If a member has knowledge or a suspicion that a client or an employer is money laundering they must report this to the Serious Organised Crime Agency (SOCA).

- The maximum penalty if convicted of money laundering is 14 years imprisonment.

- Failure to report carries a maximum penalty of 5 years imprisonment or a fine.

- Accountants must have training and internal procedures in place to ensure that they comply with the legal requirements and regulations relating to money laundering.

- It is an offence to tip-off somebody who has been reported to SOCA on suspicion of money laundering.

- Before accepting a new client an accountant must obtain documentary evidence to confirm the name and the identity of a new client.

statute law	laws that are passed as acts of parliament and relate to the legal governance of the land
case law	law that has been established based upon legal decisions made in previous cases
lien	the right of an accountant to retain a client's books and records until the accountant's fees are paid
Limitation Act 1980	a statute which sets out the time limits for taking legal action
professional liability	the legal responsibility that a professional person has for work that they carry out that a client then relies on
professional negligence	this may occur where a client, to whom the member owes a duty of care, suffers a financial loss which can be proved is the fault of the accountant
disclaimer of professional liability	a clause that an accountant includes in a document in an attempt to minimise his/her liability relating to the information provided
professional indemnity insurance	insurance that an accountant takes out to cover any damages he/she may have to pay a client due to professional negligence
money laundering	moving illegally acquired cash through financial systems so that it appears to be legally acquired
Proceeds of Crime Act 2002	a statute that sets out the law in relation to financial gains made from illegal acts
Terrorism Act (2000)	a statute that sets out the law in relation to terrorism financing
Money Laundering Regulations 2007	the regulations governing the crime of money laundering
SOCA	Serious Organised Crime Agency
tipping off	warning an individual suspected of money laundering that he/she has been reported to SOCA

Activities

7.1 (a) Ollie, a member in practice, has been asked to complete a tax return for his client, Petunia and to act as her agent when dealing with HM Revenue & Customs. The ownership of the tax return when it is complete belongs to which of the following? ✔

Ollie	
Petunia	✔

(b) Any letters sent and received to and from HM Revenue & Customs belong to which of the following? ✔

Ollie	
Petunia	✔

7.2 Which one of the following options best describes a right of lien? ✔

The right to retain possession of another's property until an obligation is paid.	✔
The right to hold on to a client's books and records after an assignment has been completed.	
The right to be retained as the client's accountant for the following year provided the fees charged remain unchanged.	

7.3 Complete the following sentence by inserting the appropriate figure.

The Limitation Act 1980 states that the time limit for legal actions under simple contract law is ....6........... years.

7.4 Breach of his/her duty to exercise reasonable care and skill by a member of the AAT means that the member may be liable to the client for which one of the following?

	✔
breach of contract and fraud	
professional negligence and breach of confidentiality	
professional negligence and fraud	
breach of contract and professional negligence	✔

7.5 Professional indemnity insurance is taken out by a member for which of the following?

	✔
insurance against a client's failure to pay the member's fees	
insurance against a client making a claim against the member for breach of his/her duty of care	✔
insurance to pay the member's legal fees if disciplinary proceedings are taken against him/her by the AAT	

7.6 Handling the proceeds of tax evasion is only a criminal offence if the amounts involved exceed £300.

True or False?

7.7 Which of the following laws directly relate to money laundering (select all that apply).

	✔
Terrorism Act 2000	✔
Limitation Act 1980	✗
Proceeds of Crime Act 2002	✔

7.8 The maximum prison sentence for an individual found guilty of money laundering is how many years? (select one of the following options)

	✔
7 years	
9 years	
14 years	✔
There is no maximum limit	

7.9 Ludo is an AAT member who works as a sole practitioner. He suspects that one of his clients who runs a DVD rental business is also selling illegally pirated copies of films.

(a) Ludo should report his suspicions to which of the following?

	✔
The police	
The AAT	
The Serious Organised Crime Agency	✔

(b) Complete the following sentence:

If Ludo chooses to discuss his suspicions with the owner of the business he
....

	✔
may be liable to disciplinary action from the AAT.	
is guilty of the criminal offence of tipping off.	✔

7.10 Advising a client in general terms about the issue of money laundering is permitted?

True or False?

7.11 Jamie, a member in practice, has presented one of his clients, Marcus, with a bill for £4,000 for accountancy work. Marcus produces £4,000 in cash from the safe in his office. What should Jamie do in this situation?

	✔
Accept the cash from Marcus in payment for his fees and deposit it in his bank account.	
Accept the cash from Marcus but immediately report him to SOCA on suspicion of money laundering.	✔
Satisfy himself that the source of the cash is not the proceeds of any sort of criminal activity before accepting it as payment.	

13/14   93%

8 Regulations of the accounting profession

this chapter covers...

This chapter details the ways in which the accounting profession is regulated through legal requirements and accounting regulations. It also looks at other methods of regulating organisations including codes of conduct and business ethics and the implications of non-compliance. Finally the chapter looks at the relationship between the AAT and the various professional accounting bodies.

Specifically it includes:

- laws and regulations which members of the AAT must comply with

- the use of watchdogs and ombudsmen to regulate industries

- the importance of business ethics and codes of conduct

- the Nolan principles on standards in public life

- the implications of non-compliance with regulations

- professional accounting bodies and their relationship with the AAT

- the role of the Financial Services Authority

COMPLIANCE WITH THE LAW

As well as complying with the AAT Guidelines on Professional Ethics, members are expected to comply with a number of different laws and regulations. Some of these are detailed below.

AAT members are expected to comply with both **civil law** and **criminal law**. This may sound obvious, and you may say, quite rightly, that everyone should not break the law. However, it is important to highlight the fact that as professional accountants, members must always consider the legal implications of decisions that they make.

Civil law is the branch of law that deals with disputes between individuals, whilst criminal law deals with crimes and their punishments as defined in legal statutes. Criminal law is sometimes referred to as 'the law of the land' ie all the laws that are in force in a country.

The AAT Guidelines are based on the laws effective in the UK and at various points make reference to legal issues. However they are not designed to give legal advice.

Where an AAT member encounters a legal issue during the course of his/her work they should seek legal advice.

There are a number of occasions in this book where we have considered the legal implications of ethical issues that may arise during the course of a member's work.

REGULATION OF THE ACCOUNTING PROFESSION

As a professional accounting body the AAT is also regulated by the Financial Reporting Council (FRC). The FRC is an independent body that oversees the regulatory activities of all the professional accountancy bodies.

There are a number of operating bodies within the FRC which are responsible for different areas. These include:

- Accounting Standards Board (**ASB**) – responsible for issuing accounting standards
- Auditing Practices Board (**APB**) – provides auditing standards and guidance
- Professional Oversight Board (**POB**) – provides independent oversight of the regulation of the accountancy and auditing professions
- Financial Reporting Review Panel (**FRRP**) – works to ensure the annual accounts of public companies and large private companies comply with relevant accounting requirements
- Accountancy & Actuarial Discipline Board (**AADB**) – responsible for operating and administering an independent disciplinary scheme for members of a number of professional accountancy bodies.

When considering ethical issues the relevant operating body is the POB.

OTHER FORMS OF LEGAL REGULATION

In addition to specific regulations governing the accounting profession the accounting and finance sector is affected by other forms of regulation. Examples of these regulations are:

The **Health and Safety at Work Act** which aims to protect workers by regulating the safety of their workplace.

The **Environmental Protection Act 1990** which is in place to control waste management and pollution, thereby protecting the environment.

These regulations are designed to cover all types of organisation not just the accounting profession. It is important to point out that regulation of the accounting profession is not limited just to accounting issues.

OTHER METHODS OF REGULATING INDUSTRIES

Whilst legal regulation is a necessity for areas such as health and safety and the environment, as we identified above, there are also other methods that are used by individual industries to regulate themselves. We will now look at some examples of how industries self-regulate.

watchdogs

Many industries will have a members' organisation which appoints an independent **watchdog**. One definition of a watchdog is:

> **'an independent person or organisation whose task it is to police a particular industry, ensuring that member companies do not act illegally'.**

One of the best recognised industry watchdogs in the UK is the Advertising Standards Authority (ASA), the independent watchdog for the advertising industry. The ASA website, www.asa.org.uk states its mission as:

> *'The Advertising Standards Authority (ASA) is the UK's independent regulator of advertising across all media, including TV, internet, sales promotions and direct marketing. Our role is to ensure ads are legal, decent, honest and truthful by applying the Advertising Codes.'*

If a member of the public believes that an advertisement in the UK is inappropriate, indecent or unethical they can contact the ASA who will then carry out an independent investigation.

Many industries in the UK have appointed watchdogs. You should investigate the industry that you work in to see if there is a watchdog.

ombudsmen

An **ombudsman** is a person appointed by the government who deals with complaints made against a company or an individual that works in a specific industry.

The Financial Ombudsman Service, for example, was established by Parliament as an independent body of experts to settle disputes between consumers and organisations (including banks) which provide financial services. This service is available free of charge and deals with over a million enquiries a year, settling over 150,000 disputes annually.

The role of the Ombudsmen is therefore very important as it maintains the integrity of the industries they represent, and, as a result, the public's confidence in the ethical values of those industries.

BUSINESS ETHICS AND CODES OF CONDUCT

In addition to the guidance on professional ethics published by professional bodies, many organisations will have their own code of **business ethics.** These set out the rules of conduct and values that govern decisions and actions within that individual organisation. This code is designed to help an individual in an organisation, faced with an ethical dilemma, to make the right choice between alternative courses of action. It also ensures that there is consistency in the conduct of all employees within the organisation.

Each company will include different elements which it considers are important in its code of business ethics. Examples of areas on which they may give guidance include:

- compliance with the law
- competing fairly
- how to act with integrity in all business dealings
- treating suppliers, partners and customers properly
- treating co-workers respectfully
- contributing to a healthy, safe and secure workplace
- respecting the environment and contributing to the community
- respecting human rights
- maintaining high standards of financial record-keeping and reporting

If you research business ethics, codes of conduct or codes of practice in your organisation you may well find a written policy that includes some of these points together with other areas relevant to your industry.

Where a company introduces an ethical code of conduct this is not legally enforceable and criminal sanctions cannot be imposed on employees who do not comply with the code. However, there may be elements within the code that are based on laws, which could result in a criminal prosecution. For example in the list above one of the points is 'contributing to a healthy, safe and secure workplace'. Although this could be included in a firm's code of conduct this is also regulated by the Health and Safety at Work Act.

the lending code

One example of a code of practice is the **lending code**. This is a voluntary code of practice which sets standards for financial institutions to follow when they are dealing with their personal and small business customers in the United Kingdom. The lending code provides valuable protection for customers and explains how firms are expected to deal with them day-to-day and in times of financial difficulties.

The 'I DO BEST' model

Ethical codes of conduct are designed to give guidance to members on the appropriate way to deal with ethical dilemmas that they face. Members must always act professionally in the workplace and this should be reflected in the decisions that they make.One way of summarising the ethical approach that members should take is the 'I DO BEST' model shown below:

> As a member **I** have a professional responsibility to take the appropriate action. When I take action over an ethical issue I must consider how I act not just what I **DO**. If I am faced with an ethical issue I must make a choice as to the **BEST** course of action.

But the need for a sense of responsibility and ethical behaviour rests not only with the individual; it is also critical for all levels of management.

tone at the top

Tone at the top refers to the ethical atmosphere that is created in the workplace by the organisation's leadership. Management's attitude to ethics will have a trickle-down effect on the employees of the company. If the tone set by managers upholds ethical values and integrity, employees will be more inclined to uphold those same values. If, on the other hand, senior management appear unconcerned with acting ethically, employees will be more likely to feel that ethical conduct is not a focus within the organisation. Employees pay close attention to the behaviour and actions of their bosses, and they follow their lead.

The following example illustrates a situation where the tone at the top is important in an organisation

example

Jonathan works for Excelsior limited, a company that supplies and fits curtains and blinds. During a sales team meeting the company's sales manager, Rebecca Grey presented her method for maximising sales revenue. She explained that when she visits customers she assesses how much money she thinks they have and changes the price that she will charge them accordingly. She also increases the price to certain customers so that she can offer them 'big discounts' and still make a profit. She encouraged all her team to do the same.

Rebecca's selling techniques are not ethical but as she is the boss she is setting the tone at the top within Excelsior and her sales team are likely to follow her lead and sell in the same unethical manner.

the Nolan principles

So far we have looked at the importance of adhering to organisational and professional values, codes of practice and regulations. One of the key reports that has been produced in recent years relating to this area is Lord Nolan's report from his committee on standards in public life. Appointed in 1994 by the then Prime Minister, John Major, to investigate the activities of individuals working in the public sector, Lord Nolan produced the first report of his Committee on Standards in Public Life in 1995. He set out what he called 'The Seven Principles of Public Life', often described as 'the Nolan Principles'.

The Nolan Principles are:

Selflessness   holders of public office should act solely in terms of the public interest. They should not do so in order to gain financial or other benefits for themselves, their family or their friends.

Integrity   holders of public office should not place themselves under any financial or other obligation to outside individuals or organisations that might seek to influence them in the performance of their official duties.

Objectivity   in carrying out public business, including making public appointments, awarding contracts, or recommending individuals for rewards and benefits, holders of public office should make choices on merit.

Accountability   holders of public office are accountable for their decisions and actions to the public and must submit themselves to whatever scrutiny is appropriate to their office.

Openness   holders of public office should be as open as possible about all the decisions and actions they take. They should give reasons for their decisions and restrict information only when the wider public interest clearly demands.

Honesty   holders of public office have a duty to declare any private interests relating to their public duties and to take steps to resolve any conflicts arising in a way that protects the public interest.

Leadership   holders of public office should promote and support these principles by leadership and example.

We can see from the seven principles the need for ethical behaviour is relevant in all aspects of life, both in the public sector and the private sector.

NON COMPLIANCE

Failure by an individual to comply with regulations and codes of practice may result in that person being disciplined. If we take the AAT Guidelines on Professional Ethics as a key example of this – if a member is found not to have complied with the Guidelines he/she may be guilty of misconduct and subject to disciplinary action. The AAT has published Disciplinary Regulations for Members which set out the processes and sanctions that the AAT can carry out if a member is accused of non-compliance and consequently of bringing the reputation of the AAT into disrepute.

An outline of the process detailed in these regulations is set out here.

- **Disciplinary investigation** – when the AAT receives or initiates a complaint that cannot be resolved informally, an initial enquiry will be commenced to establish the facts and circumstances of the alleged breach. During this investigation the member has the right to make a written response within 21 days.

  If, after the initial enquiry, the AAT still believes the potential misconduct needs to be investigated, an investigation team will be set up which will make further enquiries.

- **Decision and recommendation** – the investigation team will consider any matters that are relevant to the investigation and then make a decision whether disciplinary action should be taken. If appropriate, they will then make a recommendation as to what disciplinary action should be taken. A full list of disciplinary action that can be taken against a member is shown below:
  - give a written undertaking to refrain from continuing or repeating the misconduct in question
  - be fined a sum of money not exceeding a maximum figure set by the AAT
  - be reprimanded
  - be severely reprimanded
  - have his/her fellow member status removed (if applicable)
  - be declared ineligible for a practicing licence
  - have his/her practising licence withdrawn
  - have his/her membership suspended
  - be expelled from the AAT

  The severity of the discipline will depend on how serious the misconduct is deemed to be.

- **Member's response** – the member can respond within one month from the date of the notice sent to him/her showing the action to be taken. He/she can either consent to the recommendation or refuse. The results of the investigation will then be published.

■ **Disciplinary tribunal** – if the member refuses his/her consent to the recommended disciplinary action it will be referred to a Disciplinary tribunal which will hold a hearing to determine what action to take.

ACCOUNTING BODIES

There are a number of accounting bodies that operate in the UK and that have an impact on the AAT. We will now look at some of these.

Consultative Committee of Accountancy Bodies

The major professional accountancy bodies in the UK and Ireland joined together in 1974 to form the Consultative Committee of Accountancy Bodies which now has six members:

■ The Institute of Chartered Accountants in England and Wales (ICAEW)

■ The Institute of Chartered Accountants of Scotland (ICAS)

■ The Institute of Chartered Accountants in Ireland (ICAI)

■ The Association of Chartered Certified Accountants (ACCA)

■ The Chartered Institute of Management Accountants (CIMA)

■ The Chartered Institute of Public Finance and Accountancy (CIPFA)

The CCAB provides a forum in which matters affecting the accounting profession as a whole can be discussed and co-ordinated and enables the profession to speak with one voice on important matters.

You will notice that the AAT is not a member of the CCAB. However, four of the accounting bodies that are members are also sponsoring bodies of the AAT. These are:

■ ICAEW

■ ICAS

■ CIMA

■ CIPFA

As AAT sponsoring bodies they work closely with the AAT to ensure a consistent approach to accounting work and also to facilitate members' progression from AAT to qualification as a professional accountant.

International Federation of Accountants

The International Federation of Accountants (IFAC) is the global organisation for the accountancy profession. It has 159 member bodies and associates spanning 124 countries and represents more than 2.5 million accountants worldwide. Its independent standard setting boards develop international standards on ethics, accounting and auditing. It also issues guidance to support professional accountants in business, small and medium practices, and developing nations.

As members of the IFAC, professional accounting bodies in the UK have a duty to uphold the ethical principles of the IFAC and follow its ethical guidelines. Like the professional accounting bodies that are members of the IFAC, the AAT has chosen to model its own Guidelines on Professional Ethics closely on those of the IFAC.

FINANCIAL SERVICES AUTHORITY

So far we have looked at the professional bodies, committees and regulators of the accounting profession. However, there are other professional bodies that have an indirect influence on the accounting profession. One of the key examples of this is the Financial Services Authority (FSA).

The FSA is the financial regulator for the UK. Its powers have been given to it by the Financial Services and Markets Act, 2000 (FSMA). It is accountable to the Treasury and therefore to Parliament, although it is entirely independent and receives no government funding. The FSA is entirely funded by the firms that they regulate.

In simple terms this means that banks, building societies, insurance companies and any other businesses offering financial services within the UK are required under the FSMA to pay fees to the FSA. This allows the FSA to effectively regulate the financial services industry as a whole.

The FSA uses a wide range of rule-making, investigatory and enforcement powers to fulfil the statutory objectives that have been detailed in the FSMA. The aim of the FSA is to promote efficient, orderly and fair financial markets which in turn will help to ensure that high ethical standards are maintained.

Chapter
Summary

- AAT members are expected to comply with both civil and criminal law and must consider the legal implications of the decisions that they make.

- Professional accounting bodies including the AAT are regulated by the Financial Reporting Council (FRC) which is made up of a number of different operating bodies.

- In addition to specific regulations governing the accounting profession there are other general regulations that all organisations must comply with including the Health and Safety at Work Act and the Environmental Protection Act.

- Industries self-regulate by appointing watchdogs and ombudsmen.

- Many businesses have their own business ethics and codes of conduct which help individuals in the organisation to make the right choice when faced with an ethical dilemma.

- Individuals who work in an organisation will be influenced by the management's attitude to ethics; the tone at the top will have a trickle down effect on all the people who work for it.

- The seven principles of public life set out in Lord Nolan's report on standards in public life are:
  - selflessness
  - objectivity
  - openness
  - leadership
  - integrity
  - accountability
  - honesty

- If an individual fails to comply with regulations and codes of conduct he/she may be disciplined. For example, a member who does not comply with the AAT Guidelines on Professional Ethics may be guilty of misconduct and subject to the AAT Disciplinary Regulations for Members.

- The Consultative Committee of Accountancy Bodies provides a forum where the accounting profession as a whole can discuss accounting matters and speak in one voice on important matters.

- The four sponsoring bodies of the AAT are:
  - Institute of Chartered Accountants in England and Wales
  - Institute of Chartered Accountants of Scotland
  - Chartered Institute of Management Accountants
  - Chartered Institute of Public Finance and Accountancy

- The International Federation of Accountants represents 159 accounting bodies across the world. It sets standards on ethics, accounting and auditing and issues guidance and support to professional accountants worldwide.

- There are other professional bodies that have an indirect influence on the accounting profession; the key example of this is the Financial Services Authority. The FSA is the financial regulator for banks, building societies, insurance companies and all other businesses offering financial services in the UK.

Key Terms	**civil law**	the branch of law that deals with disputes between individuals
	criminal law	legal statutes that deal with crimes and their punishment
	Financial Reporting Council	the FRC is an independent body that regulates the accounting profession
	Health and Safety at Work Act	legislation which aims to protect workers by regulating the safety of their workplace
	Environmental Protection Act 1990	legislation to control waste management and pollution to protect the environment
	watchdog	an independent person or organisation whose task is to police a particular industry, ensuring that member companies do not act illegally
	ombudsman	someone appointed by the government to deal with complaints made against an industry
	business ethics and codes of conduct	guidelines drawn up by individual organisations which set out its values and governs decisions and actions within that organisation
	tone at the top	the ethical atmosphere that is created in the workplace by the organisation's leadership
	the Nolan principles	seven principles set out by the Nolan Committee to maintain standards in public life
	Disciplinary Regulations For Members	sets out the processes and sanctions that the AAT can carry out if a member is accused of non-compliance with the AAT Guidelines on Professional Ethics
	Consultative Committee of Accountancy Bodies	a forum in which matters affecting the accounting profession as a whole can be discussed
	International Federation Of Accountants	the IFAC is the global organisation for the accounting profession which has 159 member bodies and represents more than 2.5 million accountants worldwide
	Financial Services Authority	the FSA is the financial regulator of all businesses offering financial services in the UK

Activities

8.1 The AAT Guidelines on Professional Ethics are an example of civil law.

True or False?

8.2 (a) The independent body that oversees the regulatory activities of professional accounting bodies is called the FRC.

Which of the following does FRC stand for?

Financial Regulatory Council	
Financial Reporting Committee	
Financial Reporting Council	✓

(b) Which part of the FRC is directly responsible for reviewing the way in which professional accounting bodies in the UK regulate their members?

The Accounting Standards Board (ASB)	
The Professional Oversight Board (POB)	
The Financial Reporting Review Panel (FRRP)	✓

8.3 An ombudsman is normally appointed by the government.

True or False?

8.4 The Advertising Standards Authority is an example of which of the following?

An Ombudsman	
A Watchdog	✓
A Government Department	

8.5 (a) Introducing an ethical code of conduct is a legal requirement on an organisation.

True or False?

(b) Complete the following sentence by selecting the appropriate option.

Business ethics of an organisation are designed to help an individual in the organisation to
....

decide to whom in the organisation to refer an ethical problem.	✔
make the right choice in an ethical dilemma.	

8.6 Senior Managements' attitude to ethics is sometimes referred to as which of the following?

The 'I Do Best' model	✔
The tone at the top	
The ethical code of conduct	

8.7 Identify which three of the following business values are set out in the Nolan Principles.

Transparency	
Integrity	✔
Honesty	
Accountability	✔
Truthfulness	✔

8.8 Yvonne, a member of the AAT has not complied with the AAT Guidelines on Professional Ethics.

Complete the following sentence by selecting the appropriate words from the selection below.

Disciplinary action will be taken against Yvonne if her conduct reflects .... on the

.... of the AAT.

favourably	**reputation**
other members	**adversely**

Answers to activities

CHAPTER 1: PRINCIPLES OF PROFESSIONAL ETHICS

1.1 The AAT Guidelines apply to all of the options.

- Full AAT members
- Student members of the AAT
- Members who work in practice
- Members who are employed in industry

1.2 Rendering personal services to the highest standards of conduct and performance

1.3 Continuing Professional Development

1.4 Trustworthiness

1.5 Basing decisions on real facts rather than being influenced by personal beliefs or feelings is following the fundamental ethical principle of **objectivity**.

1.6 Integrity and Confidentiality

CHAPTER 2: OBJECTIVITY AND PROFESSIONAL COMPETENCE

2.1 B. Look at the objective that is to be achieved and focus on that objective

2.2 Independence

2.3 Members of the AAT should be both independent of **mind** and independent in **appearance**.

2.4 False

2.5 True

2.6 Fairly, honestly and in accordance with professional standards so that the information will be understood in context.

2.7 Explain to Clive that he is not prepared to accept the job unless all invoices are correctly accounted for.

2.8 When he/she has a problem resolving ethical conflicts a member of the AAT should **take legal advice or contact the AAT Ethics Advice Line**.

2.9 Where a member is faced with an ethical conflict is important that he/she keeps **written records**.

2.10 Assess, Plan, Action, Evaluate

CHAPTER 3: CONFIDENTIALITY AND TAXATION SERVICES

3.1 False

3.2 False

3.3 It is acceptable to disclose confidential information in the following situations:

- where there is a professional duty to disclose
- when disclosure is required by law
- when authorised by the client or employer

3.4 No. Richard should not provide Juliette with this information as it is confidential.

3.5 Obtain written authorisation from the client to allow you to provide the bank with this information.

3.6 To move illegally acquired cash through financial systems so that it appears to be legally acquired.

3.7 A member of the AAT has a professional duty to disclose confidential information to protect his/her **professional** interests in **legal proceedings.**

3.8 It is not kept for more than three months.

3.9 Notification

3.10 True

CHAPTER 4: ETHICS AND THE EMPLOYED ACCOUNTANT

4.1 Whistleblowing

4.2 The Public Interest Disclosure Act 1998

4.3 Professional negligence

4.4 She will be protected provided she acts in good faith.

4.5. Ralph can still carry out the project if **his employer makes sure that he has adequate support**.

4.6 The risk of loss resulting from **inadequate** or **failed** internal processes, people and systems or from external events.

4.7 False – it will increase the operational risk

4.8 Inducement

4.9 Take legal advice and inform the AAT of the offer.

CHAPTER 5: INDEPENDENCE OF THE MEMBER IN PRACTICE

5.1 • statutory external audit
• investment business

5.2 AAT members are required be to independent of **assurance** clients.

5.3 This situation presents a potential **self-interest** threat to Samantha's independence.

5.4 Self-review threat

5.5 An advocacy threat to a member's independence may occur when a member **promotes** a client's **position** to the point that his/her future **objectivity** may be compromised.

5.6 (a) objectivity and confidentiality

(b) Ensure each client is fully informed of the circumstances to allow them to make an informed decision.

5.7 A policy never to enter into an arrangement with a client who has any kind of business relation with an existing client.

5.8 Give the money to the client unless the client agrees that Jenifer should keep it.

5.9 Members of the AAT should not enter into any activities that may bring the reputation of the AAT into disrepute.

5.10 Fraud by failing to disclose information.

5.11 Hold Rose's money separately from his personal money and the business's money.

5.12 False – unless it has been pre-agreed with the client.

CHAPTER 6: TAKING ON NEW CLIENTS

6.1 Names of all the staff who will be working on the assignment

6.2 True

6.3 **Contingent** fees mean that the client will only pay the accountant if the work results in the agreed outcome.

6.4 False, this is an acceptable way of calculating fees

6.5 Professional Clearance letter

6.6 Defamation

6.7 • Verify Caroline's identity
• If Caroline has a business partner, verify his/her identity

6.8 If a member chooses to compare his/her practice with other accountants he/she must be totally **unbiased** and must be able to **prove** that what is being said is **true.**

6.9 The client is fully aware of this arrangement

6.10 This is misleading as they only have one overseas client

6.11 Promising to undercut any quote from another firm in the area by 30%

CHAPTER 7: LEGAL CONSIDERATIONS

7.1 (a) Petunia

(b) Petunia (as she is the client and Ollie is acting as her agent)

7.2 The right to retain possession of another's property until an obligation is paid.

7.3 The Limitation Act 1980 states that the time limit for legal actions under simple contract law is **six** years.

7.4 Breach of contract and professional negligence.

7.5 Insurance against a client making a claim against the member for breach of his/her duty of care.

7.6 False – the value of criminal property involved has no bearing on reporting a money laundering offence and there is no lower limit.

7.7 Terrorism Act 2000

Proceeds of Crime Act 2002

7.8 14 years

7.9 (a) The Serious Organised Crime Agency

(b) If Ludo chose to discuss his suspicions with the owner of the owner business he **is guilty of the criminal offence of tipping off.**

7.10 True – this would only be an issue if the member suspected the client of money laundering as this could be seen as tipping off.

7.11 Satisfy himself that the source of the cash is not the proceeds of any sort of criminal activity before accepting it as payment.

CHAPTER 8: REGULATIONS OF THE ACCOUNTING PROFESSION

8.1   False

8.2   (a) Financial Reporting Council

(b) The Professional Oversight Board (POB)

8.3   True

8.4   A Watchdog

8.5   (a) False

(b) Business ethics of an organisation are designed to help an individual in the organisation to **make the right choice in an ethical dilemma**.

8.6   The tone at the top

8.7   Integrity, Honesty, Accountability

8.8   Disciplinary action will be taken against Yvonne if her conduct reflects **adversely** on the **reputation** of the AAT.

Appendix

This is an example of a letter of engagement that an accountant would send out to a client before commencing an assignment. In this case the assignment is for the preparation of the year-end accounts for AKL Home Improvements.

The content of a letter of engagement can vary widely depending on the nature of the assignment. For example, the letter of engagement for a tax client would refer to the fact that the accountant was acting as an agent for the client.

It is also worth noting that different accounting practices will vary the wording of the letter of engagement that they send to the client, depending on their preferred style, but the sections covered should be broadly the same.

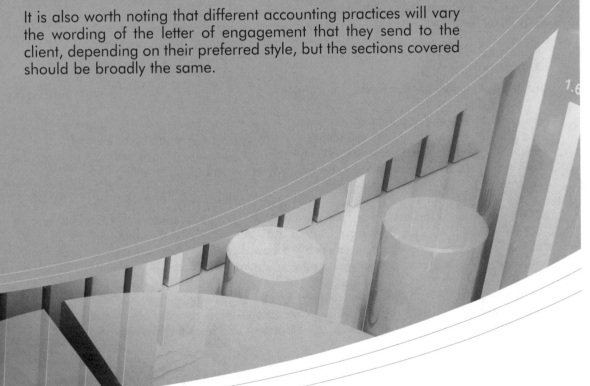

LETTER OF ENGAGEMENT

Dear Client,

The purpose of this letter is to set out the basis on which **Jacques and Khan Accountants** are engaged as your accountants and the respective responsibilities of yourselves and us.

Nature of the assignment

You have instructed us to prepare your financial statements for the year(s) ended 30th September, 2009, and subsequent years. The next section covers the detailed responsibilities that we undertake.

Responsibilities of the accountants

1.1 We shall compile the annual accounts based on the accounting records maintained by you and the information and explanations given to us by you. We shall compile draft annual accounts for your approval. We shall plan our work on the basis that no report is required by statute or regulation for the year, unless you inform us in writing to the contrary.

1.2 Our work as the compilers of the annual accounts will not be an audit of the accounts in accordance with Auditing Standards. Consequently our work will not provide any assurance that the accounting records or the accounts are free from material misstatement, whether caused by fraud, other irregularities or error.

1.3 We shall report, with any variations that we consider may be necessary, that in accordance with your instructions, we have compiled without carrying out an audit, the accounts from the accounting records of the business and from the information and explanations supplied to us.

1.4 We have a professional duty to compile accounts which conform to generally accepted accounting principles. Where we identify that the accounts do not conform to accepted accounting principles, or if the accounting policies adopted are not immediately apparent, this will be made clear in our report, if it is not clear in the accounts.

1.5 As part of our normal procedures we may request you to provide written confirmation of any information or explanations given to us orally during the course of our work.

Your responsibility

2.1 You have undertaken to make available to us, as and when required, all the accounting records and related financial information necessary for the compilation of the accounts. You will make full disclosure to us of all relevant information. The accounts need to be approved by you before we are able to issue our report.

2.2 You are responsible for ensuring that, to the best of your knowledge and belief, financial information, whether used by the business or for the accounts, is reliable. You are also responsible for ensuring that the activities of the business are conducted honestly and that its assets are safeguarded, and for establishing arrangements designed to deter fraudulent or other dishonest conduct and to detect any that occurs.

2.3 You are responsible for ensuring that the business complies with the laws and regulations applicable to its activities, and for establishing arrangements designed to prevent any non-compliance with laws and regulations and to detect any that occur.

Timetable

A private company is required to file its accounts at Companies House within 10 months of the year end. The company will be liable to a fine if it fails to do so. In order to avoid this we will produce statutory accounts suitable for filing, within the required period, provided all your records are complete and presented to us within six months of the year end, and all subsequent queries are promptly and satisfactorily answered.

Fees

Our fees are computed on the basis of time spent on your affairs and the responsibility and skill involved by the partners and staff of this firm. Unless otherwise agreed, our fees will be billed at appropriate intervals during the course of the year. Unless specifically agreed, payment of our invoices is due within 7 days from the date of the invoice.

Interest will be charged on all overdue debts at the rate stated on the invoice, which is currently ....% (APR...........%) [or, at the rate for the time being applicable under the Late Payment of Commercial Debts (Interest) Act 1998, whichever is the higher].

Ownership of records

In the event of non-payment of our fees for services rendered, we may exercise a particular right of lien over the books and records in our possession and withhold the documents until such time as payment of our invoice is received in full.

Commissions or other benefits

In some circumstances, commissions or other benefits may become payable to us in respect of introductions to other professionals or transactions we arrange for you, in which case you will be notified in writing of the amount, the terms of payment and receipt of any such commissions or benefits.

Any commission received will be paid to you.

File destruction

Whilst certain documents may legally belong to you, unless you tell us not to, we intend to destroy correspondence and other papers that we store which are more than seven years old, other than documents which we think may be of continuing significance. If you require the retention of any document, you must notify us of that fact in writing.

Ethical guidelines

We are bound by the ethical guidelines of the Association of Accounting Technicians and accept instructions to act for you on the basis that we will act in accordance with those ethical guidelines.

Clients' monies

We may, from time to time, hold money on your behalf. Such money will be held in trust in a client bank account, which is segregated from the firm's funds.

If the total sum of money held on your behalf exceeds £2,000 for a period of more than 2 months, or such sum is likely to be held for more than 2 months, then the money will be placed in an interest-bearing client bank account. All interest earned on such money will be paid to you. Subject to any tax legislation, interest will be paid gross.

If there are grounds to suspect (even if we do not actually suspect) that any monies held in a client account is derived directly or indirectly from any criminal activity whatsoever, we may not release such monies until we receive permission to do so from SOCA.

Third Parties

All accounts, statements and reports prepared by us are for your exclusive use within your business or to meet specific statutory responsibilities. They should not be shown to any other party without our prior consent.

No third party shall acquire any rights pursuant to our agreement to provide professional services.

Applicable Law

This engagement letter shall be governed by, and construed in accordance with, English law. The Courts of England shall have exclusive jurisdiction in relation to any claim, dispute or difference concerning the engagement letter and any matter arising from it. Each party irrevocably waives any right it may have to object to an action being brought in those Courts, to claim that the action has been brought in an inconvenient forum, or to claim that those Courts do not have jurisdiction.

Disclaimer

We will not be liable for any loss suffered by you or any third party as a result of our compliance with the Anti Money Laundering Legislation or any UK law or at all.

Agreement of terms

Once it has been agreed, this letter will remain effective, from one appointment to another, until it is replaced. We shall be grateful if you could confirm in writing your agreement to these terms by signing and returning the enclosed copy of this letter, or let us know if they are not in accordance with your understanding of our terms of engagement.

Yours sincerely

P Jacques   *I Khan*

For Jacques and Khan Accountants

I/We agree to the terms of this letter

A K Liennt

Signed for:

AKL Home Improvements

Date: *1 April 2010*

Index

for your notes